D1707500

WINNING THE WAR OF WORDS

WINNING THE WAR OF WORDS

Selling the War on Terror from Afghanistan to Iraq

Wojtek Mackiewicz Wolfe

PRAEGER SECURITY INTERNATIONAL
Westport, Connecticut • London

Library of Congress Cataloging-in-Publication Data

Mackiewicz Wolfe, Wojtek, 1973–
    Winning the war of words : selling the war on terror from Afghanistan to Iraq /
Wojtek Mackiewicz Wolfe.
        p.   cm.
    Includes bibliographical references and index.
    ISBN 978-0-313-34967-6 (alk. paper)
    1. Communication in politics—United States.   2. United States—Foreign
relations—2001—Public opinion.   3. Public opinion—United States.   4. Bush,
George W. (George Walker), 1946–   5. War on Terrorism, 2001–   I. Title.
    JA85.2.U6M33 2008
    973.931—dc22   2007040814

British Library Cataloguing in Publication Data is available.

Library of Congress Catalog Card Number: 2007040814
ISBN-13: 978-0313-34967-6

First published in 2008

Praeger Security International, 88 Post Road West, Westport, CT 06881
An imprint of Greenwood Publishing Group, Inc.
www.praeger.com

Printed in the United States of America

The paper used in this book complies with the
Permanent Paper Standard issued by the National
Information Standards Organization (Z39.48-1984).

10   9   8   7   6   5   4   3   2   1

To My Wife

Contents

Illustrations

Preface

psych turn

THE MAIN RATIONALE behind this book is to explain how actors can and do exploit the public's cognitive biases in order to sell risky foreign policies. This book is unique because it presents a contemporary explanation of how the policy elite used threat and loss framing to mobilize domestic support for war. The debate surrounding this issue is increasing as scholars such as Gelpi, Feaver, and Reifler posit a more gains-oriented approach to presidential framing of war.

Presidential framing sets the foreign policy tone for the American public. One would be hard pressed to argue that the president's framing of foreign policy events has no effect on the American people. The main question is what type of framing and rhetoric are effective in persuading the American public to support risky foreign policy?

To answer that question, this study explains the marketing strategy behind the war on terror and demonstrates how that strategy compelled public opinion toward supporting the spread of the war on terror from Afghanistan to Iraq. The evidence also presents a link between real-world events and theoretical explanations of the delicate relationship between foreign policy and public opinion. This investigation used qualitative methods to investigate how President George W. Bush's initial framing of the September 11, 2001 attacks provided the platform for the creation of early public support for U.S. action in Iraq and established long-term public support for the war on terror. Presidential framing of the war on terror continued to show an enduring ability to influence public support. Even two years after the U.S.-led invasion of Iraq, 52 percent of Americans believed that the United States should stay in Iraq until it stabilizes. This finding bypasses agenda-setting explanations, which prescribe issue salience among the public for only one year.

The empirical evidence in this study supports an alternative explanation in contrast to the current scholarly war and public opinion literature claiming the public's willingness to accept risks when faced with gains. Through the application of prospect theory, this study's findings hold significant implications for the understanding of sources of foreign policy formation and public support for war. The results question the rationality of public opinion in the short term, during foreign policy formation, but recognize the rationality of public opinion in the long term. The study utilizes public opinion data and nearly 1500 presidential speeches over a four-year period to empirically support the argument that presidential framing of threats and losses, not gains, contributed to public support for war in Afghanistan, war in Iraq, and President Bush's successful reelection campaign.

Acknowledgments

I AM TRULY blessed to receive help and advice from so many people throughout the three-year span of this project. I would like to thank all my friends and colleagues who offered their valuable time and advice, but first, I must thank my family for their patience and generous support throughout the entire process.

I would like to thank my parents, Bruce and Ewa Wolfe, for their unwavering love and support, which has always been a great comfort. Also thanks to Dr. Yiu and Christina Leung, for their kind generosity, their confidence, and for being my cheerleaders. Thanks to Annette Leung Evans for providing beneficial writing advice; this made a significant difference in the various revisions. Also, thanks to Larry and Linda Giebelhaus for their help and encouragement throughout the years. Thanks to Chad and Brandi Gatlin for their support. A huge thanks to John Fry and Ota Ulc, my two best friends that supported me throughout the years.

I would like to thank my dissertation chair Colin Dueck. First, I have to thank him not only for giving me the opportunity to tell this story, but also for teaching me how to tell a story. His patience through the many changes to this project and his willingness to allow me the latitude to chart its direction provided the basis for its successful completion.

I am very grateful to Steve Chan, whose advice continues to be invaluable. His difficult but honest challenges not only increased my understanding of social science but also contributed to a better final product. I am honored to have had the benefit of his mentoring.

Thanks to David Leblang for his continued support on this project and throughout the graduate studies program. Thanks to Joe Jupille for his help at a crucial time in the completion of the project. Gerard Hauser's input on the dissertation and his understanding of my various functional definitions of rhetoric was much appreciated.

Thanks to Mike Kanner for all of his help and support throughout my entire time at Boulder. His insights into the research process, teaching, and theory building proved extremely helpful at many critical junctures. He is a valued friend and colleague. I've also benefited from Gary Schaub's advice on this project and our many conversations about the profession. A big thanks to Tim Sisk at DU-GSIS for the post-doc, which gave me the necessary time to finish this project.

To my colleagues with whom I embarked on this journey: Anika Leithner and Murat Ozkaleli, thank you. You have both been tremendous friends and colleagues over the last seven years. I will never forget Murat's contagious optimism and Anika's help during some of the most essential times. Thanks also to Dean Springer; definitely one of the best people to bounce ideas off. Also, thanks to Julie Chernov for her buoyant cheerfulness and Monika Klimek for her insights into methods. Thanks to Sydney and E.B. for their untiring loyalty and companionship during the writing process.

Thanks to all the great folks at Praeger Security International for contributing to this project. I would especially like to thank my editor, Elizabeth Demers. Her interest in this book made this publication possible. Thanks to Linda Carr-Foster for the illustration work and to Laura Poole for the copyediting. Also thanks to Sue Wilson, the production editor, for providing a seamless path toward publication.

The biggest thanks go to my wife, Zora. Her love, patience, and wisdom helped me tremendously toward meeting the numerous challenges on this project and throughout graduate school. Unknowingly, many of my students also thank her for presenting me with a unique perspective on the art of teaching, which I continue to appreciate and develop.

For any individuals that I may have forgotten to mention, please accept my thanks and gratitude for your help on this project.

1

Introduction

Fear
sold the
war

GEORGE W. BUSH publicly announced during his 2000 election campaign and throughout his first eight months in office that he sought to promote a more retrenched foreign policy during his tenure in office; he intended to avoid the type of open-ended humanitarian and nation-building military engagements pursued by his predecessor. The United States was enjoying a decade of unipolar superpower status since the fall of the Soviet Union, and Bush's approach to foreign policy showed signs of defensive posturing and selective engagement. Yet in spite of this initially defensive approach, after the attacks executed by substate actors on September 11, 2001, the president and much of his Cabinet shifted from a defensive to an offensive approach focused on preemptive use of force, eventually leading to U.S. invasions in Afghanistan and Iraq.[1] The Bush administration's shift from selective engagement to primacy represented a significant shift in risk propensity while America's relative position in the world system remained unchanged, even after the September 11 attacks.[2] This inquiry will argue that the president utilized framing effects and threat rhetoric in order to successfully accomplish risky foreign policy shifts. While the administration may not have been under risk, they presented a situation to the public that implied a need for decisions to be made under risk or uncertainty, allowing prospect theory to be applied to the president's framing of the issues.

This investigation looks at the relationship between presidential framing and public support for the president and his war policies. In doing so, this study posits that the president used prospect theory tenets as a form of political communication and persuasion. While some of the president's communication can be accounted for as agenda setting, a framing explanation seeks to explain more specifically how the president not only changed the subject of foreign policy debate but also pushed his foreign policies toward successful policy execution. It is precisely in the foreign policy arena that the president has such a significant amount of room to maneuver in presenting and executing foreign policy options. This study does not imply that the president or his advisors had a grasp of prospect theory. Rather, they were lay practitioners of prospect theory's underlying concepts, which are a part of human psychology.

The operating assumption of this study is that rhetoric plays a role in a politician's ability to create consensus among the populace[3] and is supported by the idea that "a discourse of indignation, threat and suffering . . . communicated within a group, can become the basis for mobilization against an identifiable enemy."[4] However, while this study does not purport that presidential framing is the sole causal factor in building support for war, framing is considered to be the main causal variable. Without rhetorical framing, it would be impossible for any policy maker to present a case for war. Consequently, this is an exploration into the causal relationships between changes in presidential framing and public support for the president and his war policies. These relationships show distinct trends and patterns in setting the public agenda and creating a type of brand recognition for certain foreign policies. This study finds that President Bush's public communications on foreign policy went through an evolutionary process that created a salient and resilient theme, the war on terror, which resonated with the American public and concomitantly with exogenous events such as the September 11 attacks, mobilized public support for foreign policy changes against Afghanistan and Iraq (Figure 1.1).

The framing and loss rhetoric timeline illustrates the development of the more powerful themes at critical decision-making junctures for the policy makers. The simple but highly effective war on terror theme helped shape the public's understanding of Operation Enduring Freedom in Afghanistan, gained support for the invasion of Iraq, and eventually helped President Bush frame the continued

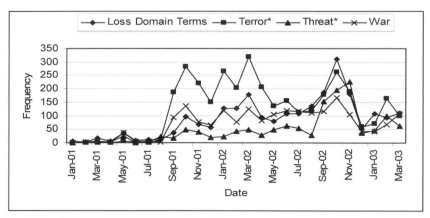

Figure 1.1   Framing and Loss Rhetoric Timeline

occupation and rebuilding of Iraq. Based on the evidence, the argument that presidential framing affects public support for war is highly credible. Overall, this study reveals six general findings regarding framing effects:

1. Framing attempts that result in first impressions for the audience matter and can withstand contradictory evidence.
2. While exogenous events are significant factors in gaining support for war, especially punitive war against terrorists, how an actor frames those exogenous events matters. Framing effects have added value because of the long-term salience they can create with the audience.
3. An effective thematic frame can be used over the long term on issues that may not be directly linked to the original exogenous event.
4. Thematic frames can be associated with an evaluation of gain or loss.
5. Loss framing is more prevalent prior to foreign policy execution while gain framing appears during the post policy timeframe, thereby supporting prospect theory tenets and having better explanatory value than expected utility theory.
6. The results question public opinion as a significant domestic source of foreign policy.

Throughout this study, we will see how framing and rhetoric influence changes in public opinion. The goal is to support the argument that framing creates descriptive invariance of a situation and thereby influences the audience to make a less than fully rational decision. For instance, by focusing on the threat of Iraq's potential weapons of mass destruction (WMDs) development and its possible support for terrorism, President Bush was able to link these themes together, evaluate them as potential losses, and contribute to an already existing post–September 11 rally effect. By linking Iraq with potential threats and exogenous events, President Bush successfully organized the policy debate around avoiding future losses.

Theory and Methods

THE MAIN PURPOSE of this investigation is to explain how President George W. Bush used framing and rhetoric in attempts to gain support for pursuing war in Afghanistan and Iraq. In essence, the point is to show that presidential speeches exploited the public's judgmental biases in order to set the foreign policy agenda and market risky changes from the status quo until those policies were implemented. According to prospect theory tenets, people exhibit judgment bias if they are risk-acceptant when faced with a situation framed as a loss and risk-averse when that situation is framed as a gain. This study will show that presidential rhetoric, as seen in terms of loss framing and loss domain rhetoric, has greater linkage with changes in public support for war than gain framing. In that manner, prospect theory provides a better explanation for this connection than expected utility theory. According to expected utility theory, changes in the dependent variable, public support, should correlate to changes in gain framing, and gain framing should dominate the president's public rhetoric during the marketing stages of potential policy changes. However, the evidence demonstrates that the opposite occurred.

Prospect theory represents a theoretical development that accounts for how risk attitude alters decision making and violates expected utility model assumptions. Past experiments and studies have shown prospect theory to be mostly successful in explaining decision making behavior under risk, with respect to reference points, domain, framing effects, and loss aversion.[1] This chapter will cover the relevant discussions on prospect theory, framing effects, presidential rhetoric, agenda setting, and war and public opinion.

Prospect theory research tradition has dictated that a more complete description of the evolution of prospect theory and its inherent framing effects requires an explanation of how the theory emerged as the major challenger to rational choice theory explanations of decision-making behavior.[2] As this research will show, the debate between prospect theory and rational choice theory continues. However, the debate has expanded to illustrate that psychological theories of decision making no longer simply describe errors in judgment but rather, they describe judgment in general, as it fails to meet the tenets of rationality.[3] The relevant literature is presented here in order to compare prospect theory findings with expected utility theory and its prescription that actors maximize their utility and are not swayed by descriptive invariance. Comparing these two sets of explanations is relevant because prospect theory not only systematically explains decision making under risk, it also explains deviations from normative axioms of decision making.

Prospect theory currently shows a distinct dearth of information surrounding the theory of framing effects. This study builds upon the existing body of knowledge in prospect theory in order to advance our understanding of framing effects and risk manipulation within the greater domestic constituency. An overview of the relevant framing literature will show how this investigation can contribute toward the accumulation of knowledge in the areas of political psychology and foreign policy behavior.

A discussion of presidential rhetoric as it relates to political marketing, or agenda setting, will provide an overview of the actor's chosen method of effective risk attitude manipulation. Scholars have already recognized the importance of rhetoric in presidential influence over both domestic and foreign policy decision making. However, the application of prospect theory to this area represents a new approach to assessing framing effects in presidential rhetoric. Additionally, this study also covers the topic of war and public opinion, requiring a brief discussion on the relevant literature.

PROSPECT THEORY

In 1979, Kahneman and Tversky proposed prospect theory as an alternative to expected utility theory in explaining decision making under risk.[4] As an alternative account of choice under risk, prospect theory is a psychological theory commonly considered to be a cognitive model of decision making rather than a motivational model.[5] This allows prospect theory to compete against subjective expected utility theory because it challenges the assumption that actors behave as if they were rational actors.[6]

Numerous experiments have shown that subjective expected utility theory is not a valid descriptive theory of human behavior.[7] Prospect theory shows that when actors have limited information, face risk, and fail to use rigorous analytical processes, they then face suboptimal outcomes. This is especially true when considering the outcomes of framing effects, or how initial options are presented to the actor.

Von Neumann and Morgenstern introduced expected utility theory as a normative theory of behavior, which describes not how people actually behave but how they would behave if they were following the requirements of rational decision making. By setting out a number of assumptions or axioms, decision researchers are able to compare mathematical predictions of the theory with how people actually behave. Invariance, an axiom of rational choice theory, states that the preference order of alternatives will remain the same over time regardless of how they are presented. In their seminal work, Kahneman and Tversky criticized this axiom because they were able to show how it can be systematically violated depending on how a problem was framed for the decision maker.

Rational choice theory and the expected utility model have been important to analysis of decision making because of their parsimony, their rigor, and the benefits of their assumption that actors will always try to maximize their utility.[8] Rational choice theory allows the researcher to create an abstraction of a problem by breaking the problem down to a set of alternatives and a set of outcomes with expected values that can then be compared in order to determine the actor's preference order.[9] An expected utility model is a basic cost-benefit analysis with the purpose of selecting the best option.[10] Another benefit to the observer who is trying to analyze real-world problems is how rational choice theory allows for the assumption that a group of decision makers can be observed as a single unitary actor.[11]

Criticisms of rational choice theory arise out of the fact that people do not always behave according to rational choice tenets. Rational choice does not account for human limitations, limited resources, and the resulting suboptimal outcomes.[12] Realistically, actors are not likely to have full access to all of the necessary information. These factors, combined with time and cognitive limitations, will cause the actors to exhibit bounded rationality and satisficing.[13] Therefore, actors may not always seem as though they are trying to maximize their utility, which contradicts a core assumption of rational choice theory and the expected utility model. Decisions that vary may be the result of different decision heuristics and therefore require the use of an evaluation process that can account for how people differ in their decision making, resulting in suboptimal outcomes. Furthermore, rational choice theory does not take into account the effects of risk on the decision maker or the fact that risk propensity changes among decision makers.

When the choices to be made entail uncertainty, they contain an element of risk. The expected value of a good is the value that we attach to the good, multiplied by the probability that we will actually get the good. Bernoulli understood that people's behavior violates the expected utility principle and developed the first cognitive approach to the idea that there is a systematic bias in decision making.[14] He argued that there is a decrease in marginal utility that is not accounted for by rational choice theory or expected utility theory.

Rational choice models do not pay attention to the way a decision maker's state of nature can shift or how his perception of the state of nature changes, thereby affecting risk propensity.[15] When a decision maker changes his level of risk acceptance, he also changes the variety of options that he has at his disposal; this is a difficult phenomenon to explain through expected utility theory.[16]

The issue of risk in decision making is magnified in the realm of international politics where actors decide their foreign policies.[17] Therefore, it is difficult to ignore cognitive approaches and the contributions they offer to the analysis of decision making under risk. Human decision makers are unable to act entirely in a manner that fits rational rationality assumptions. Emotions, culture, and human cognitive limitations play too large a role in decision making, especially risky decisions, for rational choice theory to be able to explain how people actually behave. Risky decisions are based on a variety of decision rules, which cause different outcomes.[18] Kahneman and Tversky developed prospect theory as a response to the fact that rational choice based models of decision making could not explain why people behave differently from the ways prescribed by normative decision-making theories.

Expected utility theory states that the probability of each outcome in risky situations is known and individuals weight the utilities of outcomes by the probabilities and choose the highest weighted term. Kahneman and Tversky found expected utility theory to be empirically incorrect on that note. The descriptive foundations of prospect theory are (1) people think about gains and losses around the reference point or their aspiration level rather than net assets; (2) individuals are risk-averse with regard to gains and risk-acceptant with regard to losses; (3) there is a reflection effect around the reference point at which the losses seem greater than gains; (4) people's sensitivity to change diminishes as they move further away from the reference point in either direction (at the same time, gains are treated differently from losses; people hate losing more than they like winning);[19] and (5) there is an overevaluation of current possessions, also called the endowment effect. This endowment effect can be strengthened by the symbolic value of political or economic assets.[20] Endowment effect is not only a challenge to expected utility theory, which assumes that preferences stay uniform; it can also have significant real-world impact. If an actor perceives a territory to be his in spirit but not in any legal sense, then he may be more risk-acceptant in acquiring that area. This type of change in preferences is a violation of rational choice tenets.[21]

Prospect theory argues that individuals evaluate outcomes with respect to deviations from a reference point rather than with respect to net asset levels, thereby making the reference point an important variable. Decision makers judge gains and losses based on their reference point, an activity that can play a crucial role in changing situations. Unlike rational choice, which takes the reference point as fixed, a tenet of prospect theory is that the reference point is established during the framing phase.[22] The framing phase can affect an actor's conceptual domain. Actors perceive values in the domains of gain and loss differently and are more sensitive to losses than to gains, which leads to loss aversion.

The political implication of loss aversion is that a negative event activates further efforts that can be risky and lead to even greater losses, regardless of the net value of assets. Loss aversion in political life may not be entirely cognitive. In domestic politics, an actor may try to increase his chances of winning a reelection campaign by introducing or continuing an inevitably failing policy abroad that may raise his popularity at home. This is also logical since an actor's losses abroad may not be on the same scale of significance as the actor's loss of image or reputation at home. Therefore, prospect theory can explain an actor's perception of his domestic gains and losses as a causal explanation of his foreign policy.

With respect to bargaining and deterrence, if loss aversion is predominant, then states defending the status quo have a greater bargaining advantage because they are willing to pay a higher price in order to avoid losses. According to prospect theory, the overall expectation is that wars and conflicts are more strongly and more commonly motivated by the desire to avoid perceived losses than by the hope of making gains. Restraint in a limited war is more likely to be broken by the side fearing significant losses. One methodological problem with this is that states take risks in the first place to prevent losses. It is interesting that in some instances, the reference point may not be the status quo; the status quo and the aspiration level can coexist at different levels. Therefore, if an actor's aspiration level represents something better, then he is automatically placing himself in the domain of loss and becomes more risk seeking in order to reach his aspiration level.[23] This factor will affect the establishment of each actor's reference point on a case-by-case basis.

FRAMING EFFECTS

The framing phase of prospect theory has received the most attention in prospect theory research mainly because it is the step that gets the ball rolling for the actor, but also because it is the only aspect of prospect theory that generates observable behavior. The most general definition of framing describes it as the way in which "individuals and groups make sense of their external environment."[24] Actors must use framing in order to organize and categorize their complex realities. Framing, in prospect theory, takes on a more constricted definition where framing is the actor's perception of potential courses of action, the outcomes associated with those actions, and the probabilities connected to those outcomes.[25] The way that information and alternative courses of action are presented affects the decision maker, who is unaware of how this violates rational choice tenets.[26]

Therefore, decision makers take in presented information through their own intuitive judgment, unaware of how framing has affected their judgment. Although decision makers can be particular in how they apply norms and habits to their intuitive judgment processes, the "*manner* in which choice problems are presented can be described systematically."[27] By assuming that each decision maker uses some type of historical experience to filter information, prospect theory researchers are able to look at this behavior as systematic for all actors without looking at each individual actor's history. Researchers assume that all actors experience varying degrees of framing effects, allowing them to code a course of action relative to the actor's reference point.

This area of research has been the least fruitful in its pursuit of producing a generalizable theory of framing. Scholars have taken three approaches to explaining framing in prospect theory: looking at an actor's overall domain, the hedonic tone of the problem, and semantic manipulations of outcome descriptors.[28] Examinations of the actor's overall domain have been popular within the prospect theory research program.[29] This approach attempts to situate the actor within the domains of loss or gain, and within prospect theory principles, thereby violating expected utility theory. Although this approach is tenuous because it requires the researcher to psychoanalyze the actor's mental state during an already passed event, it does provide for historical insight into the actor's decision-making process.

The second approach looks at the hedonic tone of a decision problem and tries to find a natural frame for a certain problem type. Research suggests that people will react naturally to certain types of problems as a result of shifts from the status quo. This shift is expected to produce a natural frame indicative of gain or loss without the need to identify a subjective frame.[30] This allows researchers to predict future decision making by identifying how specific conditions within a decision-making event affect actors. Scholars argue that this type of approach does not aid the development of a theory of framing and it counters the subjective nature of prospect theory, which stipulates different reactions for how information is presented, not how most actors will react to an objective situation. Furthermore, research has shown that hedonic tone does not have continued effect in life-and-death situations, when the actor may become more risk-acceptant as a result of the situation, regardless of the hedonic tone of the available options.[31] In those situations, hedonic tone loses explanatory value. Nevertheless, it may be possible to build meaning of loss or gain and create a hedonic tone for certain issues within the large capacity for decisions between issues of life and death.

The most difficult approach to identifying framing effects revolves around the analysis of semantic manipulations of outcome descriptors.[32] Boettcher points to a set of three criteria stipulated by Taliaferro in order to test the prospect theory hypothesis.[33] The criteria include identifying the decision maker's evaluated outcomes vis-à-vis the reference point, whether or not the decision makers perceive themselves to be facing gains or losses, and whether or not the decisions are made as predicted by prospect theory tenets. These criteria present a tall order for the researcher and as a result have had a limited following, especially outside of experimental methods in areas such as historical case studies.

Within the laboratory environment, it is possible to control for these variables by providing the test subject with a specific reference point or assessing the subject's reference point through interviews during the experiment. However, this type of clinical environment approach to testing prospect theory has been the target of numerous criticisms since it does little to apply the research program to real-world cases. In an effort to take prospect theory out of the laboratory and into the real world, it is justifiable to adjust Taliaferro's rigid criteria when looking at how presidential framing affects public opinion.

TYPES OF FRAMES

A wide variety of framing categories exist in political psychology research. Some of the frames are distinct to prospect theory research and have not been assessed in other research programs. Other types of frames may be more generally recognized outside of political science research. This study will mainly focus on one of three typologies of framing effects—risky choice framing. This type of framing best describes Kahneman and Tversky's theory that when information is encoded as either positive or negative, it affects the actor's risk attitude.[34]

This selection of framing types focuses on variance framing and ignores other types of framing effects in order to focus the explanatory value of this study on how emphasizing situational gains or losses can sway public audiences. This inherently leads the researcher to focus on gain, loss, thematic, and evaluative frames, found mainly in prospect theory literature.

While it is difficult to predict which type of framing the actor will chose to utilize most often, for the initial data analysis, the content analysis will focus on the aggregate effects of gain and loss framing as described in the theory and methods chapter. This will then lead to a more in-depth analysis of the actor's attempts to frame foreign policy issues for the public.

Gain and loss framing can influence how the audience defines situational outcomes. The basic form of a risky choice decision model involves presenting the situation as having two prospects. Those prospects can be presented in either risky terms as losses or riskless terms as gains. In most laboratory experiments, risky choice framing subjects are typically presented with both options.[35] In the political arena, politicians are more likely to accentuate one aspect of an issue, rather than offer an objective account of the foreign policy choices. By emphasizing potential gains or losses, political leaders are engaging the audience in a de facto two-person bargaining game, capitalizing on the audience's sensitivity to speech nuance. This allows national leaders "to define policy debates according to vocabulary and by using concepts favourable to their own positions."[36] Foreign policy brokers can then weigh the effectiveness of their sales pitch according to changes in public support for their policies.

Since the evidence in general supports the idea that people are more likely to accept greater levels of risk when framing focuses on avoiding future losses, then gain and loss framing can be an effective tool in presidential rhetoric and political communication. Moreover, this gives credence to the argument that prospect theory can account for political manipulation outside of an experimental environment.

Framing and political marketing go hand in hand when national leaders attempt to execute strategic manipulation in an effort to control issue outcomes. Thematic framing plays a crucial role in creating the focal lens through which an actor attempts to manipulate an audience. Thematic framing consists of focusing on policy attributes "and/or the introduction of organizing themes into the policy debate."[37] This concentrates on the importance of certain policy attributes that the leader wants to emphasize in order to gain support for the particular policy. For example, if an actor focuses on the vulnerability of existing policy and the positive security attributes of a new policy then he may gain support for a change from the status quo. Thereby the actor also succeeds in prioritizing security as an issue within the policy debate.

This can also have an effect on the public's reference point. If the public begins to view war as a way of avoiding future losses, then framing can aid in shifting the public's reference point away from the status quo and toward the domain of loss. In effect, if presidential framing focuses on potential threats, it can promote a more risk-acceptant public, willing to accept status quo–changing foreign policies.

The dependent variable in this study is public support for war, which includes support for the president; the polling data show that a significant percentage of the public lends its support for the president's foreign policies as a result of their over-all presidential approval. The independent variables are loss framing, loss rhetoric, gain rhetoric and gain framing, as measured by keywords in context analysis.

While the dependent variable is public support, we can identify the public's risk propensity according to their levels of support for future policy changes and continued support once the policy has been implemented. The public is thought to be more risk-acceptant when their support for going to war increases. When the public's support for an ongoing war diminishes, they become risk-averse.

Prospect theory has shown its value as an explanation of actors' perceptions of gain and loss in their personal and professional prospects. While numerous studies have focused on how actors' deviations from rational choice theory tenets can be explained by prospect theory, less research has been conducted on how elite actors use framing to market their foreign policies. In this sense, this study bypasses the traditional prospect theory explanation of actors' domains as explanatory variables of foreign policy decision making and diverts from mainstream prospect theory research. Rather than explain why some policies are status quo–changing while others are defensive, this study seeks to explain how actors attempt to sell and maintain risky status quo–changing policies to their domestic constituencies.

The former research proposition requires the researcher to take a tenuous leap of logic into the actors' psyche and analyze whether they consciously perceived themselves to be doing better or worse than expected and, if so, whether or not that affected their judgment. This approach creates a difficult dilemma for the researcher. First, it is highly unlikely that the researcher can gain adequate primary access to the actors themselves in order to conduct this type of psychological analysis. Second, even if access was not an obstacle, the researcher would have to assume that the actors were fully cognizant of their own mental state at the time the decision was made and could later recall those private insights. Last, the validity of the data collected would rest on the assumption that the actors were genuinely honest about their recollections.

In general, the researcher would be asking the actors to admit to the possibility that they acted irrationally and were possibly overly risk-averse or risk-acceptant in their foreign policy decisions. The likelihood of experienced elite politicians being so cognizant and forthcoming with their own mental assessments for the purposes of scholarly research may be unlikely. This leaves the researcher in a data validity dilemma requiring the use of numerous and sometimes tenuous assumptions.

Within this study, risk is defined as any change from the status quo. This assumes that wartime is not the accepted status quo, based on the expectation of war termination. A more traditional definition of risk refers to situations in which the actor has either perfect knowledge of the situation and knows the exact levels of potential risk or when the actor has incomplete knowledge of the situation and cannot make subjective probability calculations. This definition does not fit well with explaining real-world situations since actors rarely have perfect knowledge or no knowledge to the point where they cannot make any type of subjective probability calculation.[38]

A more advanced definition utilizes three indicators from the political actor's perspective, as proposed by Taliaferro.[39] The first risk indicator is the potential for divergence between two outcomes, meaning that the actor has an understanding of the potential for success or loss. This would imply that the public would understand that going into Afghanistan in 2001 the United States could either win a war against the Taliban or it could experience loss similar to the Soviet experience in Afghanistan. It is plausible that if the United States chose inaction against Afghanistan in 2001, President Bush would have faced risk with his domestic constituency. However, it is not possible to assess the president's, or in this case the public's comprehension of the risks inherent with invading Afghanistan.

Taliaferro's second and third risk indicators point to the possibility of negative outcomes and the possibility of flawed subjective probability estimates. While it is possible that the public was aware of the potential for negative outcomes to some degree, it is not feasible to assess their levels of flawed subjective utility estimates. Since the president's decision-making skills are not the dependent variable for this study and access to information to assess his knowledge of the situation is limited, both the traditional and Taliaferro's definitions of risk were abandoned in the early stages of this study.

Consequently, the more simple definition of risk, a change from the policy status quo, was adopted as it is more applicable and does not require the use of assumptions about the decision maker's state of mind. This definition fits well within the literature, especially when attempting to determine a layperson's risk assessment. For Kahneman and Tversky, risky choices such as "whether or not to go to war, are made without advance knowledge of their consequences."[40] This is because the actor does not know how the opponent will react. A layperson may have even less knowledge than an expert in inferring how the opponent will react. Moreover, the layperson is not likely to have immediate (if any) statistical evidence and will make "inferences based on what they remember hearing or observing about the risk in question."[41] Accordingly, it is plausible to assume that after September 11, presidential speeches regarding the war on terror provided a likely source for the public's information on the terrorist threat.

It is important to point out that this vulnerability to prospect theory research, and political psychology research in general, does not emanate out of the theoretical model but from the secretive nature of national security decision-making processes. This is an expected problem as prospect theory is not a theory of foreign policy making, rather, it can be used as an application to help better explain decision-making behavior. To promote further prospect theory research, it is also helpful to build upon theories and assumptions that have been recognized in other disciplines.

It is reasonable to make the assumption that experienced and successful political leaders are expert promoters, are highly adept at influencing public opinion, or have access to such advisors. We know that presidents can and do use rhetoric to control agenda setting and focus public attention on specific issues.[42] They then use political marketing to specify policies on those agendas toward successful execution. We also rely on the assumption that in a democracy, elite rhetoric is necessary to frame foreign policy options and attempt to affect public support for those policies. However, we do not have a highly recognized or systematic approach to describe how state leaders utilize public rhetoric in order to manipulate the public's risk propensity. In these cases, it is beneficial to the study of public support for war, to assess how President Bush encouraged his constituency to bypass the existing status quo and support and maintain risky foreign policies abroad.

This study will utilize prospect theory tenets in order to explain how state leaders use framing and rhetoric to market risky policy changes and shape national security choices for their audiences. Leaders rely on framing effects in public speeches in attempts to build public support for their policies and strategies by maintaining or altering the public's domain, thus affecting the public's risk propensity and gaining support for changing the status quo. Thus, effective framing can be beneficial to state leaders marketing their strategies to public audiences. Successfully altering the public's domain can be advantageous when attempting to introduce risky and aggressive security strategies, making state leaders lay practitioners of prospect theory in how they publicly spin their policies and try to influence public sentiment.

The mobilization of domestic support for larger strategies is an integral part of the security strategy implementation process.[43] In mobilizing support, actors will try to convince the domestic audience to support one of two options, maintain or change the current status quo. To preserve the status quo, the actor needs to either maintain or increase the audience's confidence in the present and future domains, thus maintaining their current risk-averse attitude. To alter the status quo, the actor must discount the utility of maintaining the current path, introduce the shadow of the future as a loss and modify the public's risk attitude to be more risk-acceptant and policy change supportive. The operational definition of risk for this study is a policy change from the existing status quo. Accordingly, the introduction or expansion of a foreign policy involving military intervention abroad would constitute a change from the status quo.

The use of thematic and evaluative frames may inject doubt and cause the audience to discount the utility of pursuing the status quo. If actors are successful in reducing the public's confidence in maintaining the status quo, then they will have greater public support for an alternative change. The public may then believe that they are avoiding future losses by deviating from the current status quo. Therefore, a change in risk attitude may be achieved by changing an audience's perceptions about the probabilities of a future threat, such as a terrorist attack involving the use of weapons of mass destruction (WMDs).

This study will contribute to the existing prospect theory literature by progressing toward a theory of presidential framing for a domestic audience, which has not been attempted within prospect theory research. More specifically, this study will assess how leaders utilize framing in their public rhetoric while marketing risky policy changes. This research approach looks beyond the individual's cognition of his own prospects and explains how prospect theory can be utilized in the public setting. The questions being answered here are: does framing change the public's support for risky changes, and when is this type of framing effective?

Surprisingly, the concept of framing is the most underdeveloped of all the prospect theory tenets, yet it has been relied upon for a wide variety of elite decision-making explanations. This study will provide a more systematic approach to better explain how national leaders mobilize domestic support for war. Although previous prospect theory research has examined the robustness of framing effects, very few have focused on the manipulation of the domestic public's domain.[44]

Another hopeful contribution to the existing international relations literature is to provide a clearer connection between presidential rhetoric and prospect theory through the use of a content analysis approach. In effect, this study claims that not only has prospect theory moved beyond the laboratory but that the political elite are lay practitioners, utilizing framing effects in their rhetoric in order to sell and maintain risky policies.

Two issues make this investigation interesting; first, this is an attempt to progress the applicability of prospect theory by taking it outside of the experimental testing laboratory and into the practitioner's arena. In the twenty-five years since the development of prospect theory, scholars have made significant progress in further development and application of the theory to international relations.[45] At the same time, critics have questioned the fruitfulness of taking a test tube theory, developed in a controlled environment, and applying it to the complex world of international politics. In addressing that issue, one of the intended purposes of this study is to contribute to an expansion of prospect theory's applicability to real-world problems by applying the theory to a set of contemporary cases.

Experimental results show that prospect theory explains decision making under risk regardless of the participants' similarities or differences. Thus, this approach should be applicable to different state leaders, with their own unique personalities and belief sets, without diminishing the descriptive potential. Successful testing of this proposition will help counter some of the criticisms aimed at prospect theory's general applicability.

The second intended outcome is to further expand and invite the use of this cognitive model of decision making to explain our complex political reality. Scholars have utilized prospect theory research to explain theoretical puzzles both in and out of the field of political science. Prospect theory has been expanded to discuss topics such as cumulative prospect theory,[46] contextual analysis,[47] deterrence,[48] and suboptimal outcomes in investment strategies.[49] Although the financial world varies in many ways from the realm of international politics, it also carries many of the complexities and risks that international relations scholars can appreciate. The use of a content analysis approach not only helps broaden the accessibility of prospect theory research beyond experimental testing, it also allows us to explain more real-world problems.

METHODS

The method of risk assessment in policy making is based on a fundamental approach. New policies that aim to change the existing status quo are considered risky, while status quo policies are considered nonrisky. Therefore, if the actor is trying to introduce new policies, he is expected to use loss framing to alter the public's domain. Conversely, if the actor is trying to maintain the status quo, then his rhetoric will contain gain framing in order to highlight the benefits of the current status quo to the public. The data collected in this study came from President George W. Bush's public speeches that mentioned foreign policy and national security issues. Since this project is focused on public rhetoric that was openly available, no information accessibility arose.

The compilation and analysis of the variety of presidential rhetoric is based on basic tenets found within prospect theory. One reason for this is the reality that presidential framing does not follow expected utility theory and cost benefit calculations. Instead, presidential rhetoric focused on loss framing events and the environment in attempts to gain support for future and current policy costs.

Content analysis of George W. Bush's rhetoric reflected the prospect theory framing argument with respect to his speeches after September 11 and during Operation Enduring Freedom in Afghanistan and the war in Iraq. While pushing his Iraq policy, Bush took advantage of loss framing right up to the actual invasion and continued to do so in attempts to establish a new aspiration level—winning the war on terror. Within each case, the frequency of thematic and loss framing showed significant increases until the peak of the postinvasion framing of the Iraq war as a necessary aspect of the war on terror.[50] The framing progression throughout each of the cases in this study helps answer the question, what constitutes successful framing with domestic audiences?

The actor's attempts to alter the public's domain through the use of framing in rhetoric were assessed through the use of content analysis derived from predicate analysis. Although this type of content analysis has not been utilized to assess domain in prospect theory, it has been used to assess conceptual domains in speech patterns.[51] The purpose of this content analysis is to link speech with changes in public opinion and subsequent foreign policy making. This unique approach contains a word checklist that can be applied to any public political actor in an open or semi-open society that utilizes public rhetoric.

The domain checklist was created a priori, rather than relying on grounded theory that dictates choosing the method of analysis after the data has been collected.[52] However, when the data included the use of metaphors, historical analogies, and framing, analysis was performed after data collection, as it was difficult to predict the actor's rhetoric.

The checklist for the gain and loss domains contains a preselected word bank for key terms synonymous with their respective domains. Using the Concordance software program, the researcher collected the listed terms from relevant public speeches. These words were then analyzed in context for their respective meanings in order to measure the intended level of gain or loss in each speech. The aggregate outcome of the predicate checklist produced a quantitative output, which was then interpreted for context. Consequently, this approach was a combination of content analysis and interpretive analysis.

Taking a more rigorous and a priori approach to content analysis would help in establishing a stronger case for method reliability. However, that type of content analysis requires a certain amount of interpretation, and the validity of this type of research is limited as it is vulnerable to researcher subjectivity.[53] Therefore, even if all of the evidence supports the argument hypothesized in this study, the conclusions need to be limited only to the selected cases.

A wide selection criterion for choosing speeches was used in order to promote a greater amount of reliability in repeated trials, a difficult undertaking especially when dealing with qualitative analysis. Accordingly, the selection criterion was simple and required that the president made mere mention of U.S. foreign policy or national security in each speech in order to include that public communication in the speech set. While this included 1458 speeches, in which some of the speech content did not focus on foreign policy, it does allow for replicability with a greater degree of reliability if attempted by another researcher.[54]

The search process consisted of selecting all publicly available speeches for each month from 2001 through 2004 and reading them individually for foreign policy content. This manual process proved more accurate than a search engine in determining whether or not each speech contained references to foreign policy or national security issues. Each speech was then edited, so only President Bush's comments are in the text, while comments from additional speakers, reporters, and other member of the administration were removed. All of the speeches used in this study are available in their original format online at www.whitehouse.gov.

The initial part of the study utilized domain keywords as search terms. The domain keywords are synonymous with the terms gain and loss (Table 2.1). This straightforward approach is intended to extrapolate Kahneman and Tversky's

Table 2.1   Gain and Loss Domain Keywords

Gain	Loss
accept, accomplish, accumulate, achieve, acquire, acquisition, addition, advance, advancement, advantage, appreciate, appreciation, approach, attain, awake, bag, benefit, blessing, boom, breakthrough, bring, buildup, capitalize, capture, carry, clear, compass, compensation, delay, derive, deserve, dividend, earn, earnings, educe, enter, familiarize, fatten, find, gain, gather, gathering, get, good, grow, growth, haul, have, hit, hope, improve, improvement, increase, incur, interest, jump, land, learn, look, make, master, mend, obtain, output, overtake, pay, perk, pick, plus, prevail, prize, proceeds, procrastinate, procure, produce, progress, prosper, pull, purchase, purpose, reach, realize, reap, receipts, receive, recover, recruit, recuperate, regain, return, revenue, reward, sake, score, secure, seize, snatch, spoils, succeed, success, take, triumph, victory, win.	bankruptcy, bottom casualty, consumption, cost, costly, death, decline, decrease, defeat, deficiency, deficit, deprivation, destruction, detriment, devastation, disappearance, expense, failure, fall, fat, fatality, forfeit, harm, havoc, hurt, injury, lack, leak, lose, loss, illness, misfortune, miss, passing, relapse, ruin, fright, toll, tied, waste, wear.

original concept of psychological domains of gain and loss into the practitioner's arena, in a parsimonious manner.[55] The keywords were taken from Roget's *New Millennium Thesaurus* and arranged into two keyword banks.[56] The terms were then used as search terms using the software.[57]

The content analysis software used in this study was the Concordance v. 3.2 Program, which allows for multiple keyword searches and provides keyword in context output. This provided the researcher the ability to confirm domain terms and framing effects as they were presented within the speech context.

This software also allowed for context analysis of each individual speech or of all the speeches within a specified time period. In each case, the aggregate data was separated by month in order to show broad trends and patterns over time. The loss and gain domain analysis was broad and general, whereas the framing analysis was more specific. Consequently, the overall analysis moved from general to specific in looking at framing effects over time.

As the analysis progressed from domain terms to framing analysis, the focus also shifted to more foreign policy–centered speeches; however, this was not an exclusive selection as the president utilized various platforms for pushing his foreign policy agenda. The framing analysis focused on any speech, remark and statement that the president used to comment on foreign policy. This selection criterion was used to avoid the inclination toward researcher bias in speech selection. In this manner, the more inclusive approach is more reliable in testing the domain keywords. The thematic and loss framing analysis requires more interpretation and produces less reliable results but allows the researcher to identify presidential framing trends.

In the interest of reliability and replicability, the loss domain analysis was based only on the terms synonymous with gain and loss. This approach will allow another researcher to conclude similar findings using the same software program, thesaurus, and speech set. The words themselves represent the most common meanings associated with the domains of gain and loss, however, this association has its limits. Some terms can be used in ways that do not clearly convey positive or negative connotations and have to be looked at in context. For example, the words *fall* and *wear* may be used to mean the season of the year and the act of wearing clothes, respectively. While wearing clothes has little meaning, in the context of "those who wear the uniform," the meaning changes.

The weakness in this type of straightforward content analysis requires looking at some of the keywords in context as well as the identification of framing attempts. At the same time, terms with dual meanings were rarely used to convey a strong and succinct threat.

To avoid reliability issues, the speeches were taken as a whole. This resulted in some speeches containing more content on domestic issues than foreign policy issues. Editing speeches individually for foreign policy content would create significant reliability issues and was not pursued.

For the keyword analysis, the data was aggregated by month and the data output listed the frequency of each set of terms according to each month and speech. As the analysis progressed, individual frames such as threat, war and terror were tracked to show changes over time, with reference to the initial status quo. This allowed the researcher to establish if and how the political leader attempted to introduce status quo-changing frames, thereby increasing or decreasing the public's risk propensity.

THEMATIC AND EVALUATIVE FRAMING

Thematic framing can also be identified as presidential content-based marketing of a situation for the public audience. This type of framing can generate greater issue salience amongst the public audience.[58] Evaluative framing is an attempt to frame a situation as either a gain or a loss. Prospect theory scholars have successfully utilized evaluative framing and shown actors' attempts to manipulate the reference point on issues by pointing to gains or losses.[59] Often, thematic and evaluative framing are combined to establish a theme as a gain or a loss. The keyword in context analysis provides a look at how the war theme was framed before and after the September 11 attacks. The following results show that prior to the attacks, President Bush typically framed war as a historical issue and evaluated it as a gain frame, with references to winning World War II and the Cold War:

> Half a century ago, the Class of '51 ventured into a world where the very existence of our nation seemed to hang in the balance. Thanks in part to their service and sacrifice, the values of democratic freedom prevailed throughout some 40 winters of a Cold **War**.[60]

> Throughout America, we will find monuments to those who served in that **war**. The generation of World **War** II defeated one of history's greatest tyrannies, leaving graves and freedom from Europe to Asia.[61]

Gain framing of the war theme was also used when discussing the ability to fight war:

> You're entitled to a defense budget that meets our current needs and our future obligations. And you're entitled to a Commander-in-Chief who sets a clear goal, a clear vision for our military. And that goal is to be well-equipped and well-trained, to be able to fight and win **war**, and, therefore, prevent **wars** from happening in the first place. (Applause.)[62]

> To do so, we must build forces that draw upon the revolutionary advances in the technology of **war** that will allow us to keep the peace by redefining **war** on our terms. I'm committed to building a future force that is defined less by size and more by mobility and swiftness, one that is easier to deploy and sustain, one that relies more heavily on stealth, precision weaponry and information technologies.[63]

However, after the September 11 attacks, the war theme typically referred to the war on terror and framed it as a loss, with references to present and future costs:

> If you choose to go into the military, I want to thank you, and let you know that your government will stand squarely behind you. Whatever it takes to win the **war** on terror, we will pay it. (Applause.)[64]

> We've got a huge challenge against us—for us. A huge challenge, a huge hill to climb in America, winning the **war** on terror and changing the culture for the better.[65]

> I appreciate so very much the fact that the Americans from all walks of life have stepped back and have figured out that this is going to require a lot of effort and energy to succeed in our **war** against terror.[66]

> We're on a mission and we will not yield until the mission is complete. The **war** against terror is broader than just Afghanistan.[67]

> I understand the **war** on terror is going to beyond probably 2002. I have no unrealistic aspirations about a calendar, a quick calendar.[68]

> Okay. I said to the American people that this nation might have to run deficits in time of **war**, in times of national emergency, or in times of a recession. And we're still in all three.[69]

Table 2.2   Thematic Framing

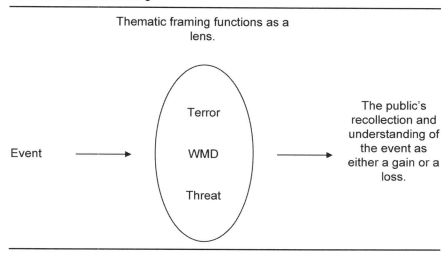

Thematic framing functions as a lens.

Event ⟶ (Terror / WMD / Threat) ⟶ The public's recollection and understanding of the event as either a gain or a loss.

The thematic framing of war included an evaluative frame and referred to current or future losses and costs. Thereby, thematic framing can be used to present a variety of organizational themes to the public and establish them as gains or losses (Table 2.2).

The thematic frame makes the public susceptible to the author's conception of an event and directs which aspects of that event become salient and how to evaluate it with respect to the status quo.[70] Therefore, an "evil Iraq" frame can mean a potential loss, while a peaceful Iraq can represent a gain. The identification of evaluation within the thematic frame is useful in tracking changes in presidential framing. This study found that some thematic frames, such as terrorism and WMDs, can carry an inherent and enduring evaluation if the initial framing was successful.

The intention was to examine specific changes in framing effects over time and link those to subsequent policy changes and trends in public opinion data. The second intention was to test the domain terms in the most reliable way possible for a qualitative approach. Overall framing trends were interconnected with foreign policy changes, exogenous events, and public opinion polls to determine if the president utilized prospect theory principles and how successful he was in affecting public support for foreign policy changes.

DATA

The loss terms are discussed in the aggregate and not according to each specific term, since the content analysis is intended to look at broad trends and the robustness of such an approach. This type of analysis differs from specific examples of thematic and loss framing, which is understood as examples of leaders framing situations and issues as better or worse than the status quo or a particular reference point.[71] Initially, it is assumed that the reference point is the current status quo until evidence shows manipulation attempts.

In limited studies, foreign policy framing has been shown to affect the audience's risk propensity through the "selective presentation of information and the semantic manipulation of outcomes (through the use of affect-laden words and phrases)."[72] This type of marketing can be used to develop support for risky foreign policies. This study will track the foreign policy frames that occurred most frequently over time. The intent is to show how certain foreign policy framing themes developed and were used to advertise a cognitive marketing brand for foreign policy issues.

The number of speeches a leader gives on a specific issue changes as foreign policy evolves; however, speech frequency does not correlate with content analysis results. Therefore, the number of speeches given is not an accurate predictor of the gain, loss, or thematic content of those speeches. One reason for speech frequency fluctuations may be the political leader's intention to communicate not only in breadth but also in depth, in order to convey the message with more emphasis. Thus, the amount of similar communication increases but is delivered outside of the major political communication arena, such as the State of the Union Address. Therefore, in times of war or during the election campaign, the leader's speech frequency increased dramatically even though the target audience of some of the speeches does not always broaden. Thus, the president has greater depth in select areas but limited breadth in communication of that message. This resulted in the same message being communicated consistently throughout the country.

Results from the domain terms indicate that loss terms showed considerable linkage to outside events and foreign policy decisions and tended to follow prospect theory tenets in that loss domain rhetoric was used to communicate policy changes or create the perception of a threatening shadow of the future (Figure 2.1).

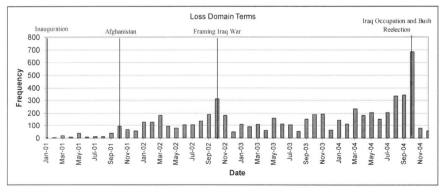

Figure 2.1   Four-Year Loss Domain Term Output

The major time periods to focus attention on in the Bush cases are first, the early months in office that showed very limited focus on foreign policy making; second, immediately after the September 11 attacks, leading up to and after the punitive war against targets within Afghanistan; and third, Bush's framing and marketing of his case for war against Iraq, which took place approximately six months prior to the actual invasion. The lag time between peak marketing of the war and actual invasion was inline with Desert Storm logistics timelines, which required approximately six months preparation prior to initiating the ground war.[73] These timeline markers are not intended as solid rules but as guidelines to direct attention to specific instances of rhetoric that link to content analysis patterns. Outside events and internal intelligence briefings do not always translate into instantaneous political rhetoric output. Some events cause quick reactions, while others take more time to develop throughout the political communication pipeline.

The time periods selected show significant fluctuations not only in loss domain rhetoric but also when looking at framing effects. Frequency in the use of threat framing and related terms increased around the September 11 attacks, the U.S. invasion of Afghanistan in October 2001, and at various times during the planning phases of the U.S. invasion of Iraq (Figure 2.2).

Conversely, the gain domain terms did not follow prospect theory tenets and did not show recognizable patterns over time. One possible conclusion may be that the gain terms may simply be more common in everyday speech than the loss terms. Possibly, their positive meaning in everyday language loses meaning in political communication. Also, it may simply be that gain framing is not as effective as loss framing, a conclusion that is supported by framing effects literature in other disciplines.[74]

It is also important to note that none of the search terms showed consistent levels of correlation with speech frequency. Thus, it is reasonable to conclude

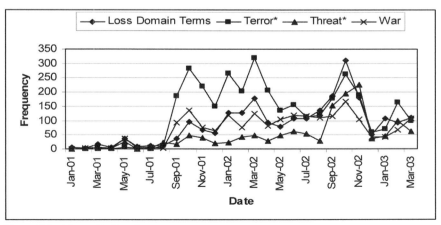

Figure 2.2   Thematic Framing

that simple speech frequency does not explain domain term results and does not show a spurious relationship with the type of speech content found in these three cases.

CASES

The cases selected for this study are intended to show the versatility of framing as a tool for domestic mobilization. The cases focus on George W. Bush from the beginning of his presidency through the September 11 attacks and Operation Enduring Freedom in Afghanistan, the lead up to the U.S.-led invasion of Iraq, and finally the subsequent occupation of Iraq.

The large amount of data, nearly 1500 speeches for the president, required a multiple case breakdown for each time case. Appropriately, the case breakdown reflects the significant timeframes related to changes in marketing the leader's foreign policy changes.

The first case began with Bush's first Inaugural Address and ended after the U.S.-led invasion of Afghanistan. It showed distinct changes in loss domain rhetoric and thematic framing pre– and post–September 11. In the immediate post–September 11 timeframe, Bush introduced a variety of thematic frames and began to push the aspiration level toward winning the war on terror, without identifying a clear timetable. Setting the reference point as an aspiration level became more helpful during the buildup to the Iraq war. As expected, there was an increase in loss framing and loss domain rhetoric in the timeframe between the September terrorist attacks and the invasion of Afghanistan. Immediately after Operation Enduring Freedom began, an increase in gain frames occurred. Although loss framing occurred in the immediate post–September 11 timeframe, it was not as ubiquitous at that point in time as it was when the president unveiled his plan to engage Iraq. Bush's post–September 11 marketing campaign appealed to a majority of Americans and thus paved the way for future foreign policy campaigns. Bush's initial September 11 thematic framing of foreign policy showed significant success in organizing and evaluating the foreign policy debate as a loss for the American public.

The second case will show how Bush utilized framing and rhetoric toward successfully marketing his case for war against Iraq. This was the most effective test in comparing prospect theory against expected utility theory as Bush made the case for preemptive rather than punitive war. Bush increased his use of loss framing and organized the policy debate according to threat and terror themes, which became even more useful during his subsequent reelection campaign. In making the case for war in Iraq, Bush's framing of Iraq as a threat to the United States and as a terrorist state dominated his public rhetoric, and his framing of Iraq as part of the war on terror resonated with the American public.

The third case covered the occupation and rebuilding stage of the Iraq war. President Bush used thematic framing, specifically the terror frame related to identifying future losses, to ratchet up diminishing support for the war and ultimately support for himself during an election year. By further reinforcing the idea that the war in Iraq was part of the broader war on terrorism, he generated just enough support for war to gain a slight majority in the public opinion polls, thus winning the 2004 election. Bush's execution of the postinvasion marketing campaign constituted a repackaging of his pre-Iraq invasion rhetoric, with a greater focus on framing Iraq as part of the war on terror, as expected from prospect theory tenets.

Using prospect theory to explain presidential rhetoric is a departure from existing prospect theory literature. While most research has focused on explaining the decision maker's state of mind, this approach bypasses tenuous psychoanalytical assumptions and looks at how the decision maker attempts to manipulate the audience's support for the given policy. Using empirical data derived from public speeches, this study established a more systematic approach to assessing decision makers' framing attempts to raise public support for risky foreign policies. At the same time, this study contributes toward an explanation of how state leaders successfully market risky security choices.

3

Foreign Policy, War, and Public Opinion

WHILE IN MOST countries, war and public opinion tend to go hand in hand, this is especially true for democracies as their leaders require significant levels of public support to both go to war and maintain war. Theodore Roosevelt was America's first leader to utilize the presidential bully pulpit when Congress failed to support his policies.[1] This practice has increased to the point that the president now addresses the public more directly, in effect almost bypassing Congress in attempts to garner support for war.[2] This direct link to the voters places democracies in a unique position when they attempt to introduce aggressive foreign policies. Even leaders in authoritarian regimes have recognized the potential to influence democracies' domestic audiences. Specifically, in 1990, Saddam Hussein unsuccessfully tried to sway U.S. public opinion against going to war by pointing to potential U.S. losses in what he termed the "mother of all battles."[3]

Unlike authoritarian regimes, democracies tend to pick wars that they are likely to win. At the same time, democracies are more likely to accept defeat in the face of growing public discontent.[4] In that sense, public opinion support for war goes along with public support for the president, who makes the decision to go to war. Therefore, the public is expected to reward an incumbent for a quick and successful war or punish a leader for making a poor decision regarding war.[5] However, while the war is ongoing and an evaluation of war progress is unclear, the political elite have great freedom take advantage of public rhetoric.[6] In essence, if the public cannot assess the war based on traditional evaluations and causal events such as gained territory or destroyed targets, they then look to the leader for that evaluation. In the process of doing so, the public evaluates the leader as well as the progress of the war, leading to leadership accountability.[7]

The causal arrow does not necessarily always run in one direction. In relatively earlier studies, Russett and Graham concluded that public opinion and foreign policy interact, questioning the realist unitary actor model.[8] However, they also concluded that the public responds not only to exogenous events or conditions but also to how policy elites and the media frame those events. They cited the public's remoteness on foreign and security policy issues as the reason for their vulnerability and reliance upon the media and policy elites for an interpretation of events. Public perception of trust in the information source is also a factor in the public's openness to framing and interpretation of events.

On the issue of whether or not the public cares about foreign affairs and security issues, the tendency may be to assume an ignorant populace. However, in a later study, Russett points out that although the public may not have a large depth and breadth of foreign affairs knowledge, they do "inform themselves about what they *care* about."[9] Furthermore, he argues that public opinion is stable, rational, and not entirely subject to elite manipulation.[10] However, he does not dispute his earlier work on the public's openness to media and elite framing.

Mueller counters the idea that the media plays a significant role in affecting public support for war. In comparing the Korean and Vietnam Wars, Mueller found no support for a causal relationship between the two variables, countering the popular conception that the media's biased reporting negatively affected public opinion through overly negative coverage of actions in Vietnam.[11] In both wars, Mueller found that public support led to a "rally around the flag" effect near the time of invasion and then began to drop in similar patterns, regardless of the tone of media reporting. It was not until U.S. casualty levels in Vietnam rose above Korean War levels that he found media reporting to play a role in affecting public support.[12] Mueller argues that the number of casualties suffered by friendly forces is the main factor explaining why war support begins to drop after the initial rally effect diminishes. As military action continues, casualty levels inevitably rise and public support for war decreases, leaving little to counter the effect.

One of Mueller's main findings after looking at the relationship between war and public opinion, ranging from U.S. involvement in World War I up to Kosovo, is that "the public applies a fairly reasonable cost-benefit analysis when evaluating foreign affairs."[13] This calculation then declines as casualties mount and the public develops greater reservations about the war's value. Similarly, Larson argues that the U.S. public does not display an instantaneous negative reaction when it comes to casualties. He argues that the public is less sensitive to U.S. military casualties if the leadership explains the mission's benefits along with the costs.[14] However, Larson seems to imply that during World War II, it was not just the benefits but also the potential losses that helped the public accept such high casualty rates.

Gelpi, Feaver, and Reifler take a slightly less deterministic approach to casualty sensitivity in their argument that the public's level of casualty aversion is affected by two factors: whether the public believes that the war was the right thing to do and the war's likely success.[15] In their previous work, prospective evaluations of success and importance of the mission to American foreign policy affect "casualty sensitivity across the public, civilian elites and military officers."[16] However, in a similar fashion to Page and Shapiro,[17] Gelpi, Feaver, and Reifler operate under the assumption that the public and their opinions on foreign policy are rational. In that sense, Gelpi, Feaver, and Reifler focus on the ability to induce the public's support through goal framing in order to convince the public to expend the costs of going to and maintaining war.

In a slightly similar goal-dependent fashion, Jentleson argues that the public is more likely to accept military casualties if the operation is quick and intended to restrain a state from aggressive behavior. Conversely, if the action is intended to coerce regime change, the public is not as likely to accept casualties.[18] Jentleson's approach looks at the public's risk aversion and his cases focus on smaller military incursions that never reached the casualty levels that showed significant effect for Mueller. Interestingly, while public opinion stays more supportive during short-term restraining actions, Jentleson argues that in the post-Vietnam era, the American public is willing to support coercive regime changing policies if the action will prevent harm against the United States.

In taking view of the larger overall picture within the literature, the focus on public opinion in determining foreign policy makes the assumption that public opinion plays a role as a domestic source of foreign policy making. Scholars often warn against ignoring public opinion altogether and attempt to assess the public's role in determining foreign policy.[19] Sobel argues that public opinion in foreign intervention policy is important because it constrains and sets limits on foreign policy action, but it does not create foreign policy by itself.[20] Thus, isolating the role of public opinion as a domestic variable is the overall question to answer; this touches upon the domestic sources of foreign policy debate. The *Innenpolitik* approach has risen in popularity and scholars are looking more toward domestic level variables as an explanation of state foreign policy making. However, generalizable and parsimonious theories utilizing the two-level games approach are yet to be presented. While this study does not pursue a theory of state foreign policy making, a brief discussion of this debate is necessary.

Apart from the problem of lacking generalizability, two-level approaches to international relations typically do not adequately specify how domestic variables are operationalized and how they take in systemic effects and translate them into foreign policy.[21] If domestic variables are to be analyzed as to how they influence foreign policy, they must also take into account the constraints imposed on states by the anarchic international system. Waltz argued that domestic level variables, while faintly relevant, have little to do with international outcomes when it comes to security concerns because all states, regardless of whether they are democratic or authoritarian, must function within the same international system and will therefore react similarly to the constraints placed on them.[22] Scholars have begun to look inside the state in order to explain issues such as the offense-defense balance,[23] domestic sources of state interest,[24] and domestic sources of foreign policy.[25] Some of them find evidence against the domestic sources of foreign policy behavior argument.[26]

The democratic peace hypothesis is perhaps the only strong "inside out" challenger to systemic approaches to international relations; "inside out" means that the hypothesis is mainly concerned with how domestic level variables influence state behavior.[27] However, because the democratic peace hypothesis is not a theory but a hypothesis that tries to explain specific empirical evidence, it does not satisfy its critics.

Moravcsik takes an extreme approach and argues that domestic variables take primacy over systemic variables.[28] He presents the idea of policy interdependence—that domestic policies in one state affect domestic politics in another state, taking precedence over systemic variables—as the main influence on state behavior and foreign policy. State preferences are the result of domestic policy competition, which are also affected by the availability of resources at the domestic level. Although Moravcsik makes the provocative argument that domestic variables have primacy, he does not explain how his domestic level variables, coalitions of interest groups, deal with systemic pressures.

Milner also argues that domestic politics matter because states' foreign policies are based on the results of a domestic level struggle for influence.[29] She also takes the stance that domestic variables take primacy over systemic variables in the sense that states are not concerned about relative gains but domestic variables are considered. She argues that domestic institutions vary in their amount of influence depending on where they are located on a domestic continuum. For Milner, foreign policy is the result of a domestic struggle for influence.

Debates on whether domestic variables and a rational public matter in international relations lead to further questions about the importance of presidential framing. If the public simply supports the president's decisions, then framing an issue as a loss or gain is not necessary. Additionally, if the public is truly rational in their opinions, they should not be susceptible to framing effects and instead be able to judge a foreign policy on its own merit. On the other hand, if the president needs the public's support before he can go to war, then how he frames the policy debate may have some impact on how people view the president's policy choices. While the evidence does not overwhelmingly support the claim that public opinion is fully determinate and a source of foreign policy change, it may not be completely extraneous to the foreign policy process. Therefore, it is logical to assess how the president engages in thematic and evaluative framing for the public and the effectiveness of those framing attempts.

SELLING THE AGENDA

The concept of political marketing has typically been applied to domestic politics, yet it seems highly appropriate to examine its role in the foreign policy arena since the goal of political marketing is to affect the target audience, which will then choose to support or reject certain foreign policy framing. While this study does not focus on whether or not foreign policy making is a top-down or a bottom-up process, it would be errant to completely ignore the role of domestic politics in the foreign policy arena. Furthermore, while scholars in conflict resolution studies have looked at how national leaders frame peace options, there is relatively less study dedicated to examining how national leaders market and promote their war initiatives. Realists focus on causes of war as exogenous while liberalists focus on domestic sources of foreign policy making. Neither camp opens the "black box" and looks at how leaders proceed in selling their policies to an audience that will eventually decide whether or not to reelect their national leaders.

With respect to presidential influence, this study refers to the more commonly recognized notion of agenda setting as political marketing. While presidential agenda setting is a well-established concept in political science literature, it seems that political marketing may be a more appropriate description for these cases, as marketing behavior implies the successful selling of a product. The key difference is that the former refers to prioritizing a foreign policy agenda for the public and the latter refers to framing and successfully executing those foreign policies.

The most accurate description of agenda setting comes from Baumgartner and Jones, who define the public agenda as "the set of policy issues to which the public attends."[30] Within that area, the study of presidential rhetoric has also contributed to our understanding of the capabilities and limitations that presidents have in influencing public opinion and bringing policy agendas to the forefront of public attention.

The president's ability to contribute to the agenda-setting process in foreign policy debate plays a large role in explaining that individual's ability to successfully engage in political marketing to the domestic audience. Moreover, since highlighting issue areas in public speeches raises not only awareness but also concern, manipulating public risk propensity is implicit in this type of political marketing.

The conventional definition of agenda setting typically identifies the president as one of the key sources of influence over the public agenda, especially on foreign policy issues.[31] Some scholars identify the president as a more effective agenda setter than Congress; moreover, Peake argues that on less salient issues the president is also more effective than the media in influencing agenda setting.[32] Cohen argues that on foreign policy issues, the president can influence public opinion by mentioning an issue without resorting to substantial arguments in issue-specific speeches. He finds that broad and unfocused presidential rhetoric does influence the public agenda, while issue-specific speeches have an even greater impact. However, that impact is short-lived, typically lasting only one year.

These findings help explain President Bush's sizable number of speeches that mentioned but did not focus on foreign policy issues. Many of those speeches focused on domestic issues, but eventually led to some reference regarding WMDs, terrorism, or Iraq. In addition, Cohen's findings support the frequency with which Bush injected references to foreign policy issues, backing previous findings that the president should push the agenda until it is executed.[33] If he is successful in increasing public attention, then he will also succeed in increasing public response.[34] Furthermore, Peake argues that agenda setting is effective if the president is able to direct and influence congressional and media attention to the issues of interest, which Bush was able to do with the successful passing of the Iraq Resolution.[35]

Because passive rhetoric directs public focus on a particular issue, presidents are not required to make impassioned pleas in order to push their agendas. However, highly public speeches can be used to further highlight the president's agenda. In that sense, the State of the Union Address is a key opportunity for U.S. presidents to successfully highlight areas of concern related to domestic and foreign policy issues. While both domestic and foreign policy issues become salient regardless of the president's popularity, foreign policy issues tend to have slightly greater longevity.[36]

A somewhat different but related issue concerns the role of presidential rhetoric. In general, the literature on presidential rhetoric is fairly abundant; however, literature that focuses on the communication of risk through rhetoric is nearly nonexistent in political science. One area within political science that may shed light on the topic looks at how presidential rhetoric affects single issues. Although this literature is sparse and typically combines presidential rhetoric with other public sources of information such as the media, it is worth noting some of the key contributions.

Behr and Iyengar discuss specific issue agenda setting but focus on the media as the key information source for the public.[37] Cameron, Lapinski, and Riemann look at presidential rhetoric but shift their focus to negotiations between the president and Congress, without focusing on political marketing to the public audience at large.[38] In one study, Iyengar showed how issue domains such as terrorism can affect citizens' sense of responsibility to take action on an issue and support it.[39] However, his study illustrates how the public places responsibility on institutions for issue domains such as terrorism and avoids discussion of the public's risk propensity to support such issues.

The field of risk communication provides some applicable material to researching perceptions of risk but for two problems: much of the research does not apply to the political arena, and nearly none of the literature covers risk communication and framing within a single study. The only applicable study covers information regarding gain and loss framing, which mirrors data found in prospect theory research.

In medical research, Edwards and colleagues found that the way risks and benefits of treatments were presented to patients affected the patients' decisions to pursue further treatment.[40] Their two main findings show that introduction of relative risks influences patients for follow-up treatment more than the introduction of absolute risks. Their second finding shows how the use of loss framing also influences patients to pursue follow-up treatment more than gain framing. In general, their research coincides with prospect theory findings as well as with the hypothesis presented in this study, that loss framing will compel the information recipient to support a change from the status quo.

September 11 and Afghanistan

AFTER THE SEPTEMBER 11 attacks, the United States began to shift its foreign policy from a defensive to an offensive approach while its relative position in the world remained unchanged.[1] Such a shift required calculated and effective marketing of changes from the status quo. The most accessible and broadly available form of political marketing continues to be in the form of public speeches, which provide empirical indicators of marketing attempts. This case will show the early evolution of how President George W. Bush used public rhetoric and framed foreign policy in an attempt to alter the public's domain and gain support for aggressive foreign policy changes.

Each empirical chapter in this study chronologically follows the president's public rhetoric, highlighting each timeframe's significant events, changes in rhetoric, and public opinion data. The conclusion will highlight main points and discuss the relative theoretical implications for prospect theory and framing research for that timeframe. Public survey and polling questions, which are used by scholars to support causal arguments in research, will highlight the relationship between framing and public opinion data. This study utilizes existing polling data that encompasses public opinion on the U.S. president and his foreign policies. This first empirical chapter begins with George W. Bush taking office in 2001.

FROM INAUGURATION TO AFGHANISTAN

The speech set for this case includes 146 of the president's public speeches, interviews, and joint statements. This is the smallest speech set relative to the other chapters. The time range for this chapter begins with Bush's inauguration in

January 2001 and ends in December of the same year. The analysis begins with Bush's first Inaugural Address and ends after the U.S.-led invasion of Afghanistan. It includes the pre– and post–September 11 timeframes and the pre- and post-Afghanistan timeframes. A number of significant events occurred during this period: the U.S. intelligence apparatus warning of potentially imminent terrorist attacks against U.S. targets abroad and/or within the United States, the September 11 attacks, and the U.S. invasion of Afghanistan.

The analysis begins with the loss domain terms and moves into thematic framing. For the loss domain terms to register a noteworthy change, a significant shift in speech rhetoric must occur and continue for more than one month. In other words, the correlating policy focus must show both depth and breadth throughout the given speeches. Consequently, since Bush's early months in office showed little foreign affairs activity and more of a domestic policy focus, the domain data showed little fluctuation in loss rhetoric. Public survey data supports the view that prior to the September 11 attacks, domestic issues such as the economy, education, and Social Security dominated the public agenda.[2] However, certain framing themes were introduced early on. Those themes then changed over time, and those changes corresponded to changes in U.S. foreign policy.

Many of the new themes introduced to the broader public later in Bush's tenure were previously reserved for specific audiences and not the public in general. For example, prior to September 11, rhetoric focusing on national security issues was directed toward audiences at the National Defense University.[3] However, in the post–September 11 era, national security and related themes were presented to the general public. The introduction of foreign policy thematic framing brought those issues to the public's attention and then framed how they were understood by the public. In that way, the thematic framing of foreign policies plays a large role when the foreign policy decision maker attempts to market policy changes that connect to the already established thematic frame.[4] In that way, Bush's thematic framing of terrorism and WMD after the September 11 attacks played an important role when he pushed for the invasion of Iraq and expansion of the war on terror. Prior to the attacks, there was relatively little rhetoric focused on foreign affairs.

PRIOR TO SEPTEMBER 11

The loss domain rhetoric data showed some fluctuation prior to the September 11 attacks, but this was relatively small when compared to the post–September 11 results (Figure 4.1).

A peak in March focused mainly on discussion of the death tax and the U.S. economy.[5] Focus on domestic politics registered a slight rise with the loss domain terms. In May, a month after the U.S. surveillance plane incident occurred in China, the data showed a significant spike; however, the speeches that showed loss domain rhetoric did not refer directly to China or the U.S. surveillance plane

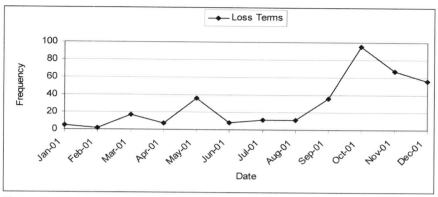

Figure 4.1   Loss Domain Graph

incident. Those speeches were directed to the National Defense University,[6] and included a presidential statement regarding domestic preparedness against WMDs.[7] While some of the speeches made references to the Cold War and the threat of mutually assured destruction, others discussed the threat of WMDs to U.S. national security. The following excerpts highlight references to the Cold War, which then transitioned into a discussion about current threats, leading to references regarding missile defense:

> We didn't trust them, and for good reason. Our deep differences were expressed in a dangerous military confrontation that resulted in thousands of **nuclear weapons** pointed at each other on hair-trigger alert. Security of both the United States and the Soviet Union was based on a grim premise: that neither side would fire **nuclear weapons** at each other, because doing so would mean the end of both nations.[8]

> In that world, few other nations had **nuclear weapons** and most of those who did were responsible allies, such as Britain and France. We worried about the proliferation of **nuclear weapons** to other countries, but it was mostly a distant **threat**, not yet a reality.[9]

Further into the speech, discussion focused onto threats from rogue states and the need for new forms of deterrence.

> Yet, this is still a dangerous world, a less certain, a less predictable one. More nations have **nuclear weapons** and still more have **nuclear aspirations**. Many have **chemical and biological weapons**. Some already have developed the ballistic missile technology that would allow them to deliver **weapons of mass destruction** at long distances and at incredible speeds. And a number of these countries are spreading these technologies around the world. Most troubling of all, the list of these countries includes some of the world's least-responsible states. Unlike the Cold War, today's most urgent threat stems not from thousands of ballistic missiles in the Soviet hands, but from a small number of missiles in the hands of these states, states for whom **terror** and blackmail are a way of life. They seek **weapons of mass destruction** to intimidate their

neighbors, and to keep the United States and other responsible nations from helping allies and friends in strategic parts of the world.[10]

Today's world requires a new policy, a broad strategy of active nonproliferation, counterproliferation and defenses. We must work together with other like-minded nations to deny **weapons of terror** from those seeking to acquire them. We must work with allies and friends who wish to join with us to defend against the harm they can inflict. And together we must deter anyone who would contemplate their use. We need new concepts of deterrence that rely on both offensive and defensive forces. Deterrence can no longer be based solely on the **threat** of **nuclear retaliation**. Defenses can strengthen deterrence by reducing the incentive for proliferation.[11]

We need a new framework that allows us to build missile defenses to counter the different **threats** of today's world. To do so, we must move beyond the constraints of the 30 year old ABM Treaty. This treaty does not recognize the present, or point us to the future. It enshrines the past. No treaty that prevents us from addressing today's **threats**, that prohibits us from pursuing promising technology to defend ourselves, our friends and our allies is in our interests or in the interests of world peace.[12]

The WMDs and threat themes were presented early on, sparingly, and to a very limited and specialized audience, yet they presented the groundwork that set the reference point on the WMDs issue: the United States was going to counter global WMDs proliferation. However, speeches that introduced this theme to the broader public did so very gradually and with extremely limited reference, beginning with the January 2001 Inaugural Address: "We will build our defenses beyond challenge, lest weakness invite challenge. We will confront weapons of mass destruction, so that a new century is spared new horrors."[13]

The introduction of this theme did not deviate from the previous administration's stance on WMDs,[14] and its mention was also brief in context of the rest of the Inaugural Address.[15] The slight reference to future losses was extremely limited. The "new horror" tag reflected a vague reference to an unknown event. No specific threat was mentioned, and no references to terrorism or national or homeland security were made in the Inaugural Address. In this pre–September 11 timeframe, the rhetoric focused on domestic nonsecurity issues, such as the economy and education.

The introduction of the WMDs theme in the pre–September 11 timeframe can be interpreted as the ideal type on the issue. An ideal type may also be presented as an aspiration level for the public that could place the public in the domain of loss on that issue, if the aspiration level is broadly accepted as a reference point. In that sense, an ideal type on WMDs can be used to manipulate the public's reference point on that issue. If eliminating ongoing WMD proliferation is the aspiration level, then it can be used to manipulate the audience into the domain of loss. By 2001, the public was well aware of WMD proliferation as a result of the media's coverage of India and Pakistan's first nuclear weapons tests, which were performed in 1998.[16] Additionally, there was increased media coverage of Russia's loose nukes and the potential for rogue nations to gain access to those weapons. However, at this point in the timeline, the mere mention of the WMDs theme in January and then later in May did not specify a particular threat.

All of the relevant themes, such as national security, homeland security, WMDs, terrorism, threat, and war, were mentioned or introduced at some point prior to September 11. The low frequencies reflected their thematic introduction, which can be used as respective reference points when compared to their post–September 11 use and development (Figure 4.2).

Looking at the thematic framing graph, we can see how little rhetorical focus was placed on security issues prior to the September 11 attacks. There was no change in frequency from June through August, even though the U.S. national security apparatus was "blinking red" with warnings of possibly imminent terrorist attacks against the United States, both domestically and abroad.[17] This indicates that during the calm before the storm, classified intelligence reports did not translate into changes in speech rhetoric in any way, an indication of the pre–September 11 frame of reference for the administration, media, and national security apparatus. At that point in time, internal intelligence briefings did not affect the content of the president's public rhetoric, which was not the case during the planning stages of the Iraq invasion. At this point in time, Bush's public approval ratings remained fairly steady, slightly around or above 50 percent, right up to the September 11 attacks (Figure 4.3).

As can be seen, the pre–September 11 communication showed little indication of the coming foreign policy changes for the United States. The themes introduced during this time did not diverge from the mainly defensive realist posturing of the previous administration. Bush's mention of the homeland security and national security themes were directed toward specific audiences of National Guard and State Department personnel, respectively, not at the American public as a whole:

As threats to America change, your role will continue to change. The National Guard and Reservists will be more involved in **homeland security**, confronting acts of terror

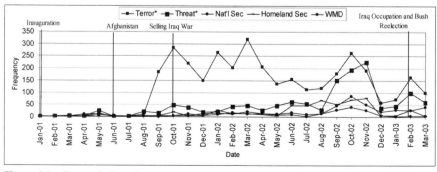

Figure 4.2   Thematic Framing

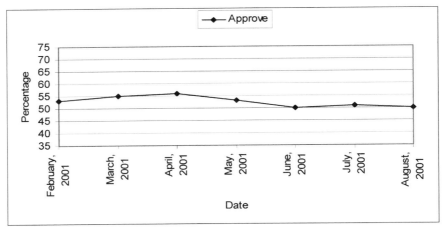

Figure 4.3   Bush Leadership Approval Index

Pew Bush Leadership Approval Index (Pew Research Center, 2005 [cited November 26, 2005]);
   available online at www.pewtrusts.com/pdf/PRC_terror_0705.pdf, www.pewtrusts.com/pdf/PRC_
   Bush_1005.pdf.

and the disorder our enemies may try to create. I welcome the important part you will
play in protecting our nation and its people.[18]

As the Secretary mentioned, I'm focusing this week on Americans' **national security**.
And few are more important to that mission than the people of the State Department,
both foreign service and civil service.[19]

This limited number of references reflected the status quo as the new administration attempted to develop an emerging national security strategy in the
post–Cold War era. The way in which these themes were framed did not include
any mention of specific threats, but instead explained a continuation of the existing mission within the U.S. national security apparatus. The lack of loss aversion
and shadow of the future references did not indicate loss framing of the national
security/homeland security themes. Accordingly, the administration was not introducing new foreign policies involving military missions abroad. In fact, the new
Bush administration was focused on reducing America's engagement in humanitarian and nation-building missions overseas and moving away from the type of
liberal internationalism promoted by the Clinton administration.[20] It is this early
context that makes the Bush administration's current posture of American primacy such an interesting agenda setting puzzle for investigation. Against the
backdrop of shifting to a more defensive realist posture, nonstate actors executed
significant attacks within the United States, thereby allowing for drastic changes
in how George W. Bush approached foreign policy changes for the next four
years.

SEPTEMBER 11 AND AFGHANISTAN

The September 11 attacks introduced a significant foreign policy shift and a change in rhetoric from the pre–September 11 months. The September and October timeframes showed new forms of thematic framing and marketing of military excursions abroad. The type of marketing used during this time period was reapplied during the build-up to the war in Iraq. The president's approval ratings experienced a rally around the flag phenomenon, which allowed for successful marketing of risky foreign policies in a very short period of time. As a result, all of the data categories rose to various degrees in September, peaked in October at the beginning of Operation Enduring Freedom in Afghanistan, and then began to decrease in November.

The loss domain rhetoric more than tripled in September and then nearly tripled again in October. The most often used loss terms in September were *hurt*, *defeat*, *destruction*, *loss*, and *death*. Loss domain rhetoric throughout the month focused on hurt businesses, hurt people, and a hurt America. Other loss domain terms pointed to the loss of lives and destruction in New York City. The following excerpts show the most frequent loss domain terms in context:

> I understand that there are some businesses that **hurt** as a result of this crisis. Obviously, New York City **hurts**. Congress acted quickly. We worked together, the White House and the Congress, to pass a significant supplemental. A lot of that money was dedicated to New York, New Jersey and Connecticut, as it should be. People will be amazed at how quickly we rebuild New York; how quickly people come together to really wipe away the rubble and show the world that we're still the strongest nation in the world.[21]

> Last week, America suffered greatly. Thousands of our citizens lost lives. Thousands were **hurt**. But thousands of our citizens rose to the occasion to help. Last week was a really horrible week for America. But out of our tears and sadness, we saw the best of America as well. We saw a great country rise up to help.[22]

> Our government is working hard to make sure that we run down every lead, every opportunity, to find someone who would want to **hurt** any American.[23]

> No, they thought they attacked America and **hurt** us. We are stronger than ever, and we will prove it to the world.[24]

> This nation stands with the good people of New York City, and New Jersey and Connecticut, as we mourn the **loss** of thousands of our citizens.[25]

> We are here in the middle hour of our grief. So many have suffered so great a **loss**, and today we express our nation's sorrow. We come before God to pray for the missing and the dead, and for those who love them. On Tuesday, our country was attacked with deliberate and massive cruelty. We have seen the images of fire and ashes, and bent steel.[26]

The following excerpts show the loss domain terms *death* and *wear* in context. This also shows the early beginnings of how the war and terror themes were eventually combined as a result of the September 11 attacks, which brought the reality of terrorist attacks to a society previously immune to such large-scale attacks from foreign terrorists:

> I've asked the highest levels of our government to come to discuss the current tragedy that has so deeply affected our nation. Our country mourns for the **loss** of life and for those whose lives have been so deeply affected by this despicable act of terror. I am going to describe to our leadership what I saw: the wreckage of New York City, the signs of the first battle of war.[27]

> Great harm has been done to us. We have suffered great **loss**. And in our grief and anger we have found our mission and our moment. Freedom and fear are at war. The advance of human freedom—the great achievement of our time, and the great hope of every time—now depends on us. Our nation—this generation—will lift a dark threat of violence from our people and our future. We will rally the world to this cause by our efforts, by our courage. We will not tire, we will not falter, and we will not fail.[28]

> Now come the names, the list of casualties we are only beginning to read. They are the names of men and women who began their day at a desk or in an airport, busy with life. They are the names of people who faced **death**, and in their last moments called home to say, be brave, and I love you.[29]

> They are the names of rescuers, the ones whom **death** found running up the stairs and into the fires to help others. We will read all these names. We will linger over them, and learn their stories, and many Americans will weep.[30]

> They put public agencies on full alert to provide immediate assistance to victims and their families; and for all those who helped, our nation is most grateful. They've called on the men and women of the National Guard to help maintain calm and order. And we thank those who **wear** the uniform as well. And they've led and supported valiant rescue workers in New York City and northern Virginia, whose bravery is seared into our national consciousness.[31]

> Secondly, we are going to dramatically increase the number of federal air marshals on our airplanes. (Applause.) When Americans fly, there need to be more highly-skilled and fully-equipped officers of law flying alongside them. Now, these marshals, of course, will **wear** plainclothes; they're going to be—they'll be like any other passenger. But Americans will know that there's more of them. And our crews will know there's more of them. And the terrorists will know there's more of them. (Applause.)[32]

The loss domain terms show specific examples of how the terrorist attacks reflected the domain of loss in comparison to the pre–September 11 timeframe, in the sense that the country and its citizens were now vulnerable to even further attacks. Prior to September 11, the president's speeches simply did not contain these references. We can see that the president is mentioning a new reference point based on the aftermath of the terrorist attacks. The discussion of the "great harm" that was done to the United States[33] and America having suffered a "great loss"[34] represents a negative change from the previous status quo. When introducing the concept of an enemy that wanted to harm the United States and Americans in general, the speaker publicly identified a specific enemy. This was the first time since taking office that the president began using loss domain rhetoric in such high frequency and toward such a broad audience.

The most often used loss terms in October were *harm, hurt, defeat, wear,* and *destruction.* The term *wear* typically referred to "those who wear the uniform." Appropriately, as the term *wear* increased in frequency, Bush addressed the nation on October 7, 2001, and announced the commencement of U.S. military strikes against al-Qaeda and Taliban targets inside Afghanistan. Interestingly, the action was not announced as a coalition effort, but as a U.S. effort aided by "our staunch friend, Great Britain. Other close friends, including Canada, Australia, Germany and France, have pledged forces as the operation unfolds."[35] The loss domain rhetoric showed discussion of the defeat and destruction of the terrorist network and enemies of the United States, mixed with what would eventually become the dominating theme in Bush's public rhetoric, the U.S.-led global war on terror.

> We will direct every resource at our command—every means of diplomacy, every tool of intelligence, every instrument of law enforcement, every financial influence and every necessary weapon of war—to the disruption and to the **defeat** of the global terror network. This war will not be like the war against Iraq a decade ago, with a decisive liberation of territory and a swift conclusion. It will not look like the air war above Kosovo two years ago, where no ground troops were used and not a single American was lost in combat. Our response involves far more than instant retaliation and isolated strikes. Americans should not expect one battle, but a lengthy campaign, unlike any other we have ever seen.[36]

> These measures are essential. But the only way to **defeat** terrorism as a threat to our way of life is to stop it, eliminate it and destroy it where it grows. (Applause.)[37]

> But we're at war, a war we're going to win. And in order to win the war, we must make sure that the law enforcement men and women have got the tools necessary, within the Constitution, to **defeat** the enemy. And there's going to be one other thing that's required to **defeat** the enemy, and that's the will and determination of the American people.[38]

> We are on a mission to make sure that freedom is enduring. We're on a mission to say to the rest of the world, come with us—come with us, stand by our side to **defeat** the evil-doers who would like to rid the world of freedom as we know it.[39]

These loss domain terms were newly injected into the public discussion, providing the framework for new and evolving thematic framing of foreign policy marketing. The association between the loss domain terms and the thematic frames introduced into the public debate supports the use of this type of content analysis in highlighting, aggregating, and relating this type of public rhetoric with prospect theory tenets. Through this content analysis approach, the researcher is able to identify associations between loss domain rhetoric, loss framing, and thematic framing, while sifting through copious amounts of data.

SEPTEMBER 11 AND SUPPORT FOR PRESIDENT BUSH

Prior to the September 11 attacks, both the president and the public focused on domestic issues, with the economy as the leading priority and President Bush's approval rating hovering around 50 percent.[40] Immediately after the attacks, Bush's approval ratings leaped to more than 80 percent with similar numbers supportive of a punitive war, 92 percent supportive of the war on terror as a multilateral approach,[41] and 85 percent supportive of a multilateral and broader campaign against terrorists beyond Afghanistan.[42] While support for the president and the war on terror most likely originated as a result from the September 11 attacks, which is considered an exogenous event, the president used rhetoric and framing to seize the opportunity to inject the war on terror theme into the public debate, beginning with the U.S.-led invasion of Afghanistan. The war on terror theme began its ascent to long-term successful thematic framing with Americans at a time when domestic public support for stronger U.S. engagement in world affairs rose to the highest levels since World War II.[43]

At the same time, 69 percent of the public supported going to war with Iraq after the completion of the war in Afghanistan. At that point in time, with such high levels of public support, two different issues require attention with respect to Americans' support for war. First, even prior to the September 11 attacks, some polls showed that a majority of Americans supported a U.S. military intervention to overthrow Saddam Hussein,[44] indicating that the potential for a war with Iraq held some preexisting resonance with the public.

Second, in the post–September 11 domain of loss, Americans not only supported the president but also believed that the United States should take a more active role in world affairs. The combination of previously existing support for war with Iraq and Americans' post–September 11 domain of loss worldview created an opportunity for the introduction of dramatic foreign policy shifts. The severity and speed of the September 11 attacks placed the American public not only in the domain of loss but in a crisis mode worldview, thereby allowing a state leader a significant policy marketing opportunity. While this level of support for war was temporary, at later points in time, President Bush attempted to recapture this level of support by extensively utilizing the global war on terror as a thematic frame in setting and maintaining foreign policy changes.

LOSS AND THEMATIC FRAMING

Both loss and thematic framing sometimes occur together; however, in the push for a punitive war against Afghanistan, loss framing was not as prevalent as in

Bush's push for war with Iraq. In discussing Operation Enduring Freedom in Afghanistan, the loss already occurred on September 11. In pushing for war with Iraq, Bush focused on future losses to successfully market a preemptive war. Because of the overwhelming support for war at the time, Bush did not need to focus on framing losses while agenda setting for the war on terror in Afghanistan. A number of Bush's post–September 11 speeches, especially the September 20 Address to a Joint Session of Congress, outlined the groundwork for the invasion of Afghanistan, under the themes of homeland security and the war on terror. All of the relevant thematic frames increased in frequency in September, peaked in October at the start of Operation Enduring Freedom in Afghanistan, and then began to drop in frequency in November once the new foreign policy was in place. At that point public discussion of homeland security and the war on terror decreased, supporting the argument that after successful policy implementation, rhetoric levels decrease to reflect high public support. The timing of the frequency peak and descent connects with Bush's limited marketing of Operation Enduring Freedom. With such high levels of support, once the policy was in place the need for policy maintenance was limited, resulting in a descent to pre–September 11 frequency levels.

Other thematic frames, such as homeland security, were not new to the U.S. national security system, but homeland security did not become part of the general public's vernacular until it was first introduced as the Office of Homeland Security in September 2001. The combination of national security and homeland security as a singular concept highlighted America's new vulnerability:

> Our nation has been put on notice: We are not immune from attack. We will take defensive measures against terrorism to protect Americans. Today, dozens of federal departments and agencies, as well as state and local governments, have responsibilities affecting homeland security. These efforts must be coordinated at the highest level. So tonight I announce the creation of a Cabinet-level position reporting directly to me—the Office of Homeland Security.[45]

The framing of the homeland security theme emphasized that America was doing worse than it should, indicative of the domain of loss, because it was framed in connection with the new threat of terrorism and the possibility of future attacks. This represented new domestic national security policy as a form of loss aversion. In that frame, very few Americans were likely to oppose such drastic domestic security changes. In fact, most citizens supported the sacrifice of some civil liberties in exchange for greater security against future terrorist attacks in 2001, and a near majority of 48 percent continues to support unwarranted eavesdropping by the government.[46] This level of support for domestic security measures may be due to the initial framing of homeland security issues, although other variables may be at play. However, historical support for the curbing of civil liberties to protect against terrorism was short-lived,[47] leaving more room to speculate on the role of initial thematic framing in maintaining public support.

In October, overall thematic framing grew in frequency and meaning as homeland security further developed as a concept intended to defend against a new threat:

> This week we established America's new Office of **Homeland Security**, directed by former Governor Tom Ridge. Americans tonight can know that while the threat is ongoing, we are taking every possible step to protect our country from danger. Your government is doing everything we can to recover from these attacks, and to try to prevent others.[48]

Highlighting an ongoing threat is an example of loss framing and loss aversion, in that it presents the homeland security concept as something that focuses on avoiding future losses as opposed to striving for future gains. The following excerpt further outlines the potential for future losses by framing the theme with discussion of evil and saving the unborn:

> This is the calling of the United States of America, the most free nation in the world. A nation built on fundamental values that rejects hate, rejects violence, rejects murderers, rejects evil. And we will not tire. We will not relent. It is not only important for the **homeland security** of America that we succeed, it is equally as important for generations of Americans who have yet be born.[49]

In the following excerpt, the speaker ties the homeland security theme to energy security: "We've spent a lot of time talking about **homeland security**. An integral piece of **homeland security** is energy independence. And I ask the Senate to respond to the call to get an energy bill moving."[50]

By framing homeland security alongside the rejection of values such as hate and evil and as the protection of unborn generations, the concept further represents the idea of loss aversion and effective loss framing of the theme. Frequently, the president piggybacked themes such as energy security with homeland and national security. Along with the increase of loss domain rhetoric, many of the speeches pointed to future losses rather than future gains. In effect, the speaker did not highlight the gains to be made by ridding the world of terrorism but focused on current and potential loss from terrorism. The peak of this rhetoric coincided with the October invasion of Afghanistan, which represented the beginning of America's foreign policy, the global war on terror. This also introduced foreign policy framing of the war on terror, using both loss and thematic frames. During this time, the frequency of the term *terror** rose from 10 hits in August to 185 in September and then 283 in October.[51]

OPERATION ENDURING FREEDOM AND THE WAR ON TERROR

Rhetoric surrounding Operation Enduring Freedom was similar to speeches related to the September 11 attacks—it focused on fighting the war on terror;

Bush outlined the military objectives of Operation Enduring Freedom in his speeches on September 20 and October 7.[52] Those objectives were centered on eliminating terrorist targets within Afghanistan in order to prevent future losses from the terrorist threat. Those speeches represent the beginning of the often-cited U.S. war on terror campaign.

Perhaps the most significant occurrence for the marketing of future policy is the joining of these two thematic concepts, war and terror, which previously led separate paths both in rhetoric and foreign policy, with *war* referring to conventional global conflict and *terrorism* referring to temporary counterterrorist policies. The joining of these concepts was sealed in the September 20 Address to the Joint Session of Congress and the American People speech, in which George Bush broke from the past and announced a continuous foreign policy against terrorism. The policy was framed as loss aversion, not as the pursuit of future gains. In this context, he proposed a long-term foreign policy change with no clear indicators of success and no visible timeline for conclusion. In a sense, the policy itself is an example of a loss rather than a gain frame because it describes a war with no end, thereby establishing an aspiration level that, if accepted, would place the American public in the domain of loss as a result of seeking to reach a possibly unattainable goal:

> Our response involves far more than instant retaliation and isolated strikes. Americans should not expect one battle, but a lengthy campaign, unlike any other we have ever seen. It may include dramatic strikes, visible on TV, and covert operations, secret even in success. We will starve **terrorists** of funding, turn them one against another, drive them from place to place, until there is no refuge or no rest. And we will pursue nations that provide aid or safe haven to **terrorism**. Every nation, in every region, now has a decision to make. Either you are with us, or you are with the **terrorists**. (Applause.) From this day forward, any nation that continues to harbor or support **terrorism** will be regarded by the United States as a hostile regime.[53]

Up until September 11, all mentions of terrorism and war were separate. Nearly all references of war were historical in nature, usually mentioned on military holidays and aimed at specific rather than general audiences. By framing war and terror as a single concept, Bush seized the moment to combine two traditionally separate forms of foreign policy. The comment that "Either you are with us, or you are with the terrorists" not only brought applause from the audience, it sealed the war on terror as a thematic frame and reflected America's new real-world loss aversion toward terrorism:

> We've just begun. There's 150 detained, and more to come. And along these lines, this weekend, through the collaborative efforts of intelligence and law enforcement, we've arrested a known terrorist who was responsible for the deaths of two U.S. citizens during a hijacking in 1986. This **terrorist**, by the name of Zayd Hassin Safarini, is not affiliated with al Qaeda. Yet he's an example of the wider **war on terrorism** and what we intend to do.[54]

And, you know, we've now got a reason to do what it takes to not only provide security at home, to do what it takes to win the **war on terrorism**, but we've also got to do what it takes to make sure this economy gets growing, so people can find work.[55]

We've got a job to do, all of us. And I'm here to thank you in the Department of Labor for your hard work, your concern for your fellow Americans. All of us, from the President all the way throughout our government, must be diligent and strong and unwavering in our determination and our dedication to **win the war on terrorism**.[56]

We had a long discussion about our mutual desire to rout out **terrorism** where it might exist. He understands as well as I understand that the **war on terrorism** will be waged on many fronts, and I'm so pleased with the efforts of his government to join with us in disrupting the financial networks of **terrorist** organizations.[57]

While it is certainly debatable whether or not these types of thematic framing helped the president market and execute Operation Enduring Freedom in Afghanistan, it is more likely that Bush's initial framing of the war on terror helped solidify the concept as a salient issue for the American public. This issue strongly resonated with the American public for the rest of 2001, when public support for the war on terror hovered between 89 and 90 percent.[58] If Bush had framed the war on terror as a cost-benefit calculation that started with September 11 and ended in Afghanistan, then it would not have been as effective in gaining support for war in Iraq. At the same time, while most framing of the war on terror pointed to losses, a limited amount of framing surrounding Operation Enduring Freedom highlighted the potential for gains. Painting a grim picture of terrorism required some color when marketing policy in a liberal democracy.

AFGHANISTAN AS A HUMANITARIAN MISSION

While more realist thematic frames emerged immediately after the September 11 attacks, one example of an idealist thematic frame is the humanitarian aid concept.[59] The thematic frame that Operation Enduring Freedom was a humanitarian mission emerged and developed alongside other security frames, to a smaller degree, but one that peaked after foreign and domestic policy changes were already implemented (Figure 4.4). There are a variety of explanations for this occurrence.

Human beings have a psychological need for a positive self-concept and a positive social or national identity. In other words, most of us like to think we are good people who do things for the right reasons. That may explain the need for rhetoric that contains both loss and gain framing in justifying war. The loss appeals to us on a rational level, that is, we want to protect ourselves, while the gain appeals to us on an emotional level, that is, we go to war to help people and spread democracy.

Psychological studies have shown that people have different identities with different needs that they constantly try to manage.[60] It is reasonable to say that parts of us are rational and therefore receptive to the discussion of loss and other parts of us are more emotional and therefore in need of a positive self-image, especially

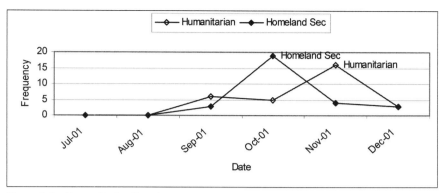

Figure 4.4   Humanitarian Framing

while doing something that is not generally considered to be positive, such as going to war.

Although this concept of gain framing may seem counter to prospect theory's findings, the timing of the more idealist humanitarian frame actually fits with prospect theory's framing effects when looking at changes in the status quo. While Operation Enduring Freedom was being planned and executed, the actor needed to prepare the public for foreign policy changes, hence the terror and loss framing. After the policy was implemented, a new status quo was established and needed reinforcement. The more idealist frame took precedence and projected a more positive image with reference to the foreign policy and its consequences. The timing of change in frames will most likely vary according to the level of support the individual leader experiences. If there is more than adequate support, then the gain frames may come earlier, prior to policy implementation. If there is limited or wavering policy support, then gain frames may be slow in coming.

Constructivists within political psychology have also shed light on the existence of gain alongside loss framing when leaders attempt to implement policy change. Shannon argues that norms are what states make of them and when leaders are faced with decisions that present a conflict between personal motivations and social constraints, then personal "biases compel leaders to interpret norms and situations in a manner that justifies violation as socially acceptable."[61] In effect, the leader has to illustrate both gains and losses in framing aggressive foreign policy changes. However, prospect theory tenets would prescribe a greater frequency in loss framing prior to successful policy implementation.

GAIN FRAMING

Gain frames associated with a cost-benefit calculation, a reasonable expectation associated with Gelpi and Feaver's argument of presenting future gains in order to persuade a defeat-phobic public, fail to gain adequate traction within the speech data.

As the self-defense or loss framing argument influences audiences toward greater acceptance of risky policy changes, international social constraints prevent leaders from continuously promoting rhetoric focused on short-term security-maximizing policies. In essence, while loss framing dominates pre-invasion rhetoric, idealist, gain, and socially acceptable frames may also be present as leaders seek to justify violation of international norms. Nevertheless, for Bush, discussion of loss through terrorism outweighed discussion of gain as a result of the new war on terror. Consequently, as the pre-invasion rhetoric of Afghanistan showed more loss frames, postinvasion rhetoric did not show a significant increase in thematic gain frames. The frequency of gain frames such as win, victory and success is minimal when compared to the terror frame (Table 4.1).

While discussion of future gains, or gain framing, did occur, it had a very limited role in the president's public rhetoric, both in frequency and in meaning:

> Americans should not expect one battle, but a lengthy campaign, unlike any other we have ever seen. It may include dramatic strikes, visible on TV, and covert operations, secret even in **success**. We will starve terrorists of funding, turn them one against another, drive them from place to place, until there is no refuge or no rest.[62]

> America and our friends and allies join with all those who want peace and security in the world, and we stand together to **win** the war against terrorism.[63]

> Behind the sadness and the exhaustion, there is a desire by the American people to not seek only revenge, but to **win** a war against barbaric behavior, people that hate freedom and hate what we stand for.[64]

> But we're at war, a war we're going to **win**. And in order to **win** the war, we must make sure that the law enforcement men and women have got the tools necessary, within the Constitution, to defeat the enemy.[65]

> All we ask is that you participate. All we ask is that you use the same amount of effort the United States will to **win** this war against freedom, to **win** this battle against global terrorism.[66]

> Fellow citizens, we'll meet violence with patient justice—assured of the rightness of our cause, and confident of the **victories** to come.[67]

Table 4.1   Frequency of Gain and Loss Evaluation Frames

Date	Terror	Threat	Victory	Win	Success
Aug-01	10	22	0	0	0
Sep-01	185	16	**7**	**32**	7
Oct-01	**283**	**48**	3	26	**14**
Nov-01	220	39	**7**	**11**	8
Dec-01	150	20	6	12	9

But as time will go on, we will know more and more about how **successful** we've been. The point is, is that we are going to be there for a while. I'm patient. The commander on the ground is executing the plan, and the American people are in strong support of what's taking place.[68]

References to winning the war on terror did not point to obvious future gains, but to a vague concept without clearly defining all of the participants. The lack of specificity in framing the war on terror policy left room for future policy expansion, which included other targets, such as Iraq.

While the idea of presenting future gains in order to promote a cost-benefit calculation by the public is logical according to expected utility, this line of logic is not evident in the speech data. The content analysis showed that discussion of terrorism and the new war on terror dominated the president's rhetoric and the public agenda. While it may not have been necessary for the president to heavily market the war on terror at that point in time, by introducing the theme in the aftermath of the September 11 attacks he solidified thematic salience and public support for future policies related to the war on terror. That initial frame played an even greater role as it evolved in later foreign policy marketing and agenda setting.

CORRELATION OR CAUSALITY?

The speech data beg the critical question of whether rhetoric had any role in affecting public support for a risky and vague policy, such as the war on terror. This research posits that a relationship between policy framing and public support is not necessarily spurious because of the constant need to advertise and maintain public support for war. Thus, while Bush may have had carte blanche to execute foreign policy immediately after the September 11 attacks, immediate framing of foreign policy after the attacks formed the foundation for future foreign policy decisions and presidential rallying in the build-up, occupation, and rebuilding of Iraq, at times with strong parallels to public support for those policies.

A variety of public opinion polls connected rhetoric framing with public support for the president and for the war on terror. The TIPP Presidential Leadership Index asked individuals their favorability levels regarding George Bush, his handling of the job as president, and the strength of his leadership. The methodology for this index indicated that a score of 50 and higher is considered to be a positive outlook. The results for this time period showed that after the September 11 attacks, opinions of Bush's leadership peaked significantly from 53.5 percent in September to 83.3 percent in October.[69] These public opinion changes showed significant relationship with changes in presidential rhetoric. Since the polls captured people's attitudes toward presidential leadership and the war on terror, there is strong evidence to support a causal relationship between President Bush's public rhetoric regarding exogenous events and how people perceived him to be handling the situation.

CONCLUSIONS

The marketing campaign executed by President Bush in the wake of the September 11 attacks paved the way for successful future foreign policy campaigns. While this study was not designed to show process learning by the practitioner, later chapters show how similar patterns of policy framing were used in sequential foreign policy marketing.

One source of recognizable disparity in framing before and after the terrorist attacks is the lack of significant foreign policy changes by the Bush administration prior to the September 11 attacks. Tacitly, the Bush administration accepted the international status quo and focused on domestic policies such as the economy and the No Child Left Behind educational policies. The lack of policy changes explains the limited amount of loss domain terms as well as the limited amount of loss framing in comparison to the post–September 11 timeframes. Therefore, comparing the pre– and post–policy implementation timeframes offers a robust pre- and posttest examination of policy marketing.

This case offers insights on three levels. First, the strong associations support the further use of content analysis on presidential rhetoric. Second, the results show that real-world framing effects and loss domain rhetoric falls in line with prospect theory's theoretical expectations, as they increased prior to the execution of a foreign policy change. Third, these results provide insight into how policy practitioners utilize certain cognitive framing concepts. Because prospect theory's theoretical findings mirror real-world events, the theory is further supported as having practical applications outside of a controlled laboratory environment. In the end, prospect theory's ability to describe and explain presidential framing of foreign policy changes provides insight into presidential attempts to rally support for war.

In the theoretical arena, this approach also provides a better explanation than expected utility theory, which should have resulted in greater frequency in gain framing of policy changes. The relative dominance of loss framing to gain framing throughout Bush's public rhetoric counters an expected utility calculation that prescribes the reliance on framing future gains in order to rally public support for policy changes. Additionally, the frequency of terror, threat, and WMDs rhetoric surpassed the frequency of winning, victory, and success rhetoric. Successful contradictory evidence would have revealed a preponderance of future gains discussions within the presidential rhetoric prior to policy execution. While the identification of gain versus loss framing has some inherent drawbacks as it falls into the researcher's subjective judgment, there was an active attempt to avoid bias by systematically searching for thematic and evaluative framing in all available speeches.

Other supportive evidence, presented in this and subsequent chapters, highlights the relationship between changes in public support and presidential rhetoric. Contradictory public opinion data would need to have shown irregular or no connection to changes in presidential rhetoric. As a result, this research provides insight into the causal relationship between presidential framing of foreign policy and the public's support for those policies.

The argument in this study posits that rhetoric and specific types of framing effects played a major role in affecting the public's support for foreign and national security policy changes. While this argument is somewhat weakened in light of the almost certain public support for punitive war immediately after the September 11 attacks, the argument gains greater traction as President Bush's foreign policy framing evolved on the road to war with Iraq.

President Bush's Road to War in Iraq

IT IS IMPORTANT to restate that in declaring war, the American president needs to have not only the support of Congress but also the support of the American people. When the president communicates on war issues, he uses persuasion within his communications.[1] Over time, presidents have used the bully pulpit to address the public more directly, in effect almost bypassing Congress in presidential attempts to garner support for war.

Campbell and Jamieson argue that throughout American history, presidential arguments for war have contained a number of recurring elements; two of these clearly occur in Bush's war rhetoric. First, the argument for war is posited within a dramatic narrative. Second, the audience is asked for a complete commitment to the cause. While Bush's rhetoric fits into some previous explanations of war rhetoric, framing effects analysis is a robust tool when looking at traditional forms of war rhetoric, such as the rhetoric geared toward war with Iraq, and less conventional war rhetoric, such as the U.S. declaration of war on terror. The main assumption driving this research presumes that presidents seek to gain significant public support prior to declaring war. Public speeches are the actor's main tool in achieving successful political communication.

This chapter examines how President Bush successfully promoted risky changes in foreign policy against Iraq. The next chapter focuses on presidential attempts to maintain that foreign policy in the face of growing costs. Certain scholars argue that the American public may be willing to accept risky foreign policy changes if they are presented as future gains with a clear strategy for success, in other words, a cost-benefit calculation.[2] Accordingly, if the public sees reasonable benefit in future victory, then the public should be willing to expend the costs of going to war. More specifically, Gelpi, Feaver, and Reifler argue that by highlighting future gains, President Bush will successfully convince Americans to expend the costs of maintaining Iraq occupation and rebuilding efforts. However, this line of thinking presumes a rational public and runs counter to prospect theory's behavioral observations, which leads toward an incongruent explanation: the public's acceptance of Bush's Iraq policy and its inherent risks and costs occurred through loss, not gain framing. To support this study's prospect theory framing effects derivative as a potential causal mechanism, this chapter will demonstrate that various forms of loss framing show a stronger connection with public opinion changes than win, victory, and gain framing rhetoric.

This chapter covers the time period from January 2002 to March 2003, which includes a number of significant policy and marketing events. Discussion of major events takes account of first, the 2002 State of the Union Address, which included Bush's previous loss and thematic framing and introduced new themes into the policy debate; second, the build-up to war in Iraq, including Bush's rallying of domestic support for the Iraq Resolution; and last, presidential framing surrounding the U.S.-led invasion of Iraq.

Possibly the most important event covered in this investigation is the president's build-up to war in Iraq. While the previous chapter explained how the president successfully marketed a punitive war in Afghanistan, this chapter focuses on how the president marketed the strategy of preemptive war and led the country into the more costly war in Iraq. Furthermore, this chapter will continue to answer a number of critical research design questions, such as whether this line of query is fruitful in determining how speech affects public opinion, and whether the explanations presented here go beyond illustrating correlation. One determinant of success is the descriptive quality and strength of the association between changes in President Bush's public speeches and changes in public support for the president and his war policies. More specifically, the issue is whether public opinion varied according to framing changes enough to support the president's decision to execute a significant change from the status quo.

Another determinant of success is whether prospect theory's explanation of public opinion is better than a cost-benefit explanation. According to the cost-benefit calculation, the speaker's public rhetoric should highlight future gains rather than future losses. The gain-oriented framing attempts should help convince the audience to accept the risks and costs of going to war. Accordingly, if President Bush managed to gain support for invading Iraq by discussing expected gains from such an endeavor, then the cost-benefit explanation would be superior. However, if loss framing dominates the speaker's rhetoric, then prospect theory's framing effects explanation would be superior for this case.

In attempting to explain the causal process behind presidential framing, this investigation argues that by quantifying speech according to prospect theory tenets and correlating it to public opinion data, we can measure presidential marketing attempts and make a case for a type of concomitant relationship. That relationship is evidenced by the public's recognition of the threat and loss concepts communicated by the president and magnified by the administration and the media. The public's recognition of those concepts is followed by variance in public opinion polls, which is then followed by changes from the foreign policy status quo.

Undoubtedly, there are a number of intervening variables that need to be explored in order to fully appreciate the complexity in this instance of risk communication, when attempting to ascertain a clearer picture of causality between the president and his constituency. However, in the interest of parsimony, it is reasonable to assume the path of travel beginning with the president and ending with the public audience, allowing the researcher to begin a series of investigations on presidential framing effects and marketing, by examining those two clearest points first.

The quantification of speech looks at the frequency of loss domain terms and thematic framing within the president's public speeches. As in the previous chapter, this section utilizes loss domain keywords that are synonymous with *loss* as search terms. This straightforward approach parsimoniously expands Kahneman and Tversky's conceptual domain of loss into the practitioner's arena.[3]

This empirical case examines President Bush's thematic and evaluative framing attempts. The domain and framing analysis used search terms within the software, which allowed for content analysis of each speech within a specified time period. The aggregate speech results are separated by month in order to show broad trends and patterns. The loss domain rhetoric analysis is broad and general, while the thematic and evaluative framing is more specific. Consequently, the overall analysis moves from general to specific in looking at framing effects over time. Analysis of public recognition and support for the president's policies follows public opinion and approval polls over the applicable timeframes. Although changes in opinion polls occur, they do not occur on a sweeping scale; it is not necessary to have overwhelming landslide public support in all policy-making situations. When public opinion changes occur on the margins, those changes may be sufficient enough to reach majority levels, allowing policy changes. While overwhelming policy support may be ideal, it is not always necessary in a winner-takes-all political system that relies on simple majority support.

Unfortunately, qualitative research presents challenges to clear and direct measurement. So evidence supportive of a causal relationship stops short of isolating the president's speeches as the only determinant in shifting public opinion. However, the evidence in this case will show that as the president framed and defined the policy debates for the audience, the public was receptive to his framing attempts and supportive of his policies. While this did not occur in broad strokes, the evidence will show that public opinion shifts occurred enough to tip toward majority support, overcoming the public's status quo bias. Support levels changed after the execution of large-scale marketing attempts. In effect, presidential policy changes followed public opinion changes. While this chain of events does not establish independent causality, the public's relative acceptance of President Bush's framing adds weight toward rejecting the null hypothesis that highlighting gains is more effective than highlighting losses in gaining public support for war policies.

Public opinion rallying effects occurring outside of exogenous events, such as terrorist attacks within the United States, represent some of the critical evidence supporting this study's argument. While presidential approval ratings rose around the September 11 attacks and the U.S. invasion of Iraq, the rally around the flag effect alone fails to explain public opinion shifts between those major events. This chapter focuses on alternative explanations of relevant public opinion shifts.

THE STATE OF THE UNION ADDRESS

The year 2002 began with President Bush continuing to receive high marks for leadership.[4] He was coming off record-high approval ratings after rallying the country in the aftermath of the September 11 attacks and ordering the ongoing but well-received operations against the Taliban and al-Qaeda targets in Afghanistan.

Accordingly, polling data showed that in January 2002, foreign affairs overtook other previously attention-grabbing domestic issues such as employment, taxes and crime. Eighty-three percent of Americans polled continued to place defending the United States from future terrorist attacks a top priority, ahead of competing domestic issues.[5] Atypically, a majority of Americans believed that the upcoming State of the Union Address would have greater importance for them than previous State of the Union speeches.

In 2002, background conditions resulting from the September 11 attacks continued to exist among Americans. Throughout the year, the public viewed terrorism as the main threat challenging the United States—more so than their second concern, a WMDs-capable-Iraq—and expected the administration to effectively prevent future terrorist attacks.[6] The upcoming State of the Union Address and expected audience interest provided the president with an opportunity to set a new policy agenda and introduce significant changes in future U.S. foreign policy. The following analysis will cover the various types of loss and gain framing, thematic framing, and loss domain results from the beginning of the year and throughout the year, leading up to the U.S.-led invasion of Iraq in March 2003. Analysis will focus on rhetoric changes correlating with policy decisions and resulting rallying effects.

The beginning of 2002 set the stage for America's change from realism to primacy in the post–September 11 era.[7] To successfully execute this change, the administration needed to deliver a well-crafted message to a captive and attentive audience. The State of the Union Address provided an ideal platform for marketing future foreign policy changes. More specifically, the address allowed for the introduction of a narrative that continued throughout Bush's war rhetoric. One of the keys to success in the president's war rhetoric was his constant and unchanging characterization of the threat, the enemies, and America's looming losses.

THREATS

In the first three sentences of his 2002 State of the Union Address, President Bush stated that the nation was at war, the economy was in recession, and the "civilized world faces unprecedented danger." The first half of the speech was dedicated to discussing U.S. vulnerability to terrorism, the extent of the terrorist threat, linking terrorism with Iraq and WMDs, and the build-up of the defense budget. The president stated three main goals for U.S. interests: "We will win this war, we'll protect our homeland and we will revive our economy." This reiterated Americans' ongoing preoccupation with post–September 11 background conditions according to the polls. With respect to prospect theory, this highlighted America's new economic and national security status quo and emphasized to the public that the country was in the domain of loss. By emphasizing America's persistent vulnerability to terrorism, Bush's rhetoric continued to frame and draw attention to potential threats.

The following excerpts from the address highlight the president's threat rhetoric, which was first introduced immediately after the September 11 attacks. President Bush's threat and terrorism rhetoric was thematically consistent throughout the State of the Union Address and his subsequent speeches:

> My hope is that all nations will heed our call, and eliminate the terrorist parasites who **threaten** their countries and our own.[8]

> The United States of America will not permit the world's most dangerous regimes to **threaten** us with the world's most destructive weapons (Applause).[9]

> And, second, we must prevent the terrorists and regimes who seek chemical, biological or nuclear weapons from **threatening** the United States and the world (Applause).[10]

Building on the rhetoric introduced after the September 11 attacks, Bush linked Iraq with the threat rhetoric by discussing it in the same context as the terrorist threat, thereby adding another dimension in defining the threat for the public:

> Our second goal is to prevent regimes that sponsor terror from **threatening** America or our friends and allies with weapons of mass destruction. Some of these regimes have been pretty quiet since September the 11th. But we know their true nature . . . Iraq continues to flaunt its hostility toward America and to support terror. The Iraqi regime has plotted to develop anthrax, and nerve gas, and nuclear weapons for over a decade. This is a regime that has already used poison gas to murder thousands of its own citizens— leaving the bodies of mothers huddled over their dead children. This is a regime that agreed to international inspections—then kicked out the inspectors. This is a regime that has something to hide from the civilized world. States like these, and their terrorist allies, constitute an axis of evil, arming to **threaten** the peace of the world.[11]

In addition to mixing Iraq with the threat rhetoric, the speaker also introduced the economic security concept by linking the federal budget with potential threats and U.S. security. By mixing the initial terrorist threat element with Iraq, the speaker added a greater depth in defining the issue:

> The next priority of my budget is to do everything possible to protect our citizens and strengthen our nation against the ongoing **threat** of another attack. Time and distance

from the events of September the 11th will not make us safer unless we act on its lessons. America is no longer protected by vast oceans. We are protected from attack only by vigorous action abroad, and increased vigilance at home.[12]

LOSSES

Manipulation of gain and loss framing persuades the audience to evaluate situational outcomes in terms of gains or losses. The basic form of a risky choice decision model involves presentation of the situation as having two prospects. Either those prospects can be presented in risky terms as losses or in riskless terms as gains. Loss framing in content analysis of presidential rhetoric cannot be interpreted as strictly as it is in a laboratory environment in order to identify framing patterns that exist in a more natural and real-world political environment. In most laboratory experiments, risky choice framing subjects are typically presented with both options.[13] However, in the political arena, politicians are more likely to accentuate either risky negative or the riskless positive aspects of an issue rather than offer an objective account of potential foreign policy choices. By emphasizing potential gains or losses, political leaders are engaging the audience in a de facto, two-person bargaining game, making the audience highly sensitive to speech nuance, including thematic framing. This allows national leaders "to define policy debates according to vocabulary and by using concepts favorable to their own positions."[14] Foreign policy actors can then weigh the effectiveness of their sales pitch according to changes in public support for their policies.

In 2002, the president introduced examples of loss framing and loss aversion when he presented the terrorism issue with a focus on avoiding future losses as opposed to striving for future gains. This rhetoric pattern was prevalent throughout 2002 and 2003, much more so than immediately after the September 11 attacks. While pushing U.S. foreign policy, Bush took advantage of loss framing right up to the U.S.-led invasion of Iraq. This was an effective communication strategy that grew as policy rhetoric evolved over time.

The following excerpts, taken from the 2002 State of the Union Address, marked the beginning of the Iraq rhetoric evolution cycle and illustrate how the administration continuously defined this foreign policy debate.

> Our cause is just, and it continues. Our discoveries in Afghanistan confirmed our worst fears, and showed us the true scope of the task ahead. We have seen the depth of our enemies' hatred in videos, where they laugh about the loss of innocent life. And the depth of their hatred is equaled by the madness of the destruction they design. We have found diagrams of American nuclear power plants and public water facilities, detailed instructions for making chemical weapons, surveillance maps of American cities, and thorough descriptions of landmarks in America and throughout the world. What we have found in Afghanistan confirms that, far from ending there, our war against terror is only beginning. Most of the 19 men who hijacked planes on September the 11th were trained in Afghanistan's camps, and so were tens of thousands of others. Thousands of dangerous killers, schooled in the methods of murder, often supported

by outlaw regimes, are now spread throughout the world like ticking time bombs, set to go off without warning.[15]

In the address, Bush defined the American fight against terrorism as ongoing and significantly greater in scope than originally expected. He listed potential U.S. targets and quantified the number of potential terrorists that could attacks those targets. Last, he argued that these terrorists could be anywhere in the world and linked their existence to state-sponsored terrorism. Reference to the ticking time bomb is symbolic and placed the issue on a time-sensitive chronology requiring immediate action. The time sensitive reference continued when defining the policy debate on Iraq. The numerous references to looming losses on the horizon due to an amplified and growing threat constitute a number of loss framing instances:

> Thanks to the work of our law enforcement officials and coalition partners, hundreds of terrorists have been arrested. Yet, tens of thousands of trained terrorists are still at large.[16]

> Our military has put the terror training camps of Afghanistan out of business, yet camps still exist in at least a dozen countries. A terrorist underworld—including groups like Hamas, Hezbollah, Islamic Jihad, Jaish-i-Mohammed—operates in remote jungles and deserts, and hides in the centers of large cities.[17]

> We can't stop short. If we stop now—leaving terror camps intact and terror states unchecked—our sense of security would be false and temporary.[18]

Bush continued framing the number and location of terrorists with vague references to actual numbers and locations. With the nineteen September 11 hijackers as a reference point, he implied that tens of thousands more terrorists existed, constituting a loss frame and further defining the debate on terrorism as an overwhelming issue. Referring to locations as anything ranging from jungles and deserts to large metropolitan areas promoted an image of potentially greater losses from future terrorist attacks when compared to the September 11 attacks, which was perpetrated by only nineteen individuals, many of whom were from Saudi Arabia.[19] The speaker also turned a sense of security into a potential loss by referring to it as false and temporary, pointing the audience to the idea that current gains against terrorism do not take the audience out of the domain of loss, but characterize the battle ahead:

> Our second goal is to prevent regimes that sponsor terror from threatening America or our friends and allies with weapons of mass destruction. Some of these regimes have been pretty quiet since September the 11th. But we know their true nature. North Korea is a regime arming with missiles and weapons of mass destruction, while starving its citizens. Iran aggressively pursues these weapons and exports terror, while an unelected few repress the Iranian people's hope for freedom.[20]

By linking the terrorism issue with sovereign states and WMD proliferation, Bush created a thematic frame defining the terrorism policy debate as one that involved rogue states, WMDs, state sponsored terrorism, and the September 11 attacks. This framing does not isolate issues into their respective policy debates but links the concepts together, creating a more ambiguous but simply understood threat.

It is important to reiterate that loss framing does not simply imply a negative connotation in speech content but also refers to potential future losses. Thus it is possible to utilize praise and positive feedback alongside loss framing and thematic framing of an issue. In the following excerpt, Bush praises current efforts and refers to current gains: "When I called our troops into action, I did so with complete confidence in the courage and skill. And tonight, thanks to them, we are winning the war on terror."[21] This was followed with a restatement of the current status quo, a progress report on the war on terror that was framed as a loss and pointed to even further losses in the future. Discussion of terrorist numbers substantially larger than the September 11 terrorists, acting under time-sensitive conditions, further compounded the loss:

> What we have found in Afghanistan confirms that, far from ending there, our war against terror is only beginning. Most of the 19 men who hijacked planes on September the 11th were trained in Afghanistan's camps, and so were tens of thousands of others. Thousands of dangerous killers, schooled in the methods of murder, often supported by outlaw regimes, are now spread throughout the world like ticking time bombs, set to go off without warning.[22]

> Our war on terror is well begun, but it is only begun. This campaign may not be finished on our watch—yet it must be and it will be waged on our watch. We can't stop short. If we stop now—leaving terror camps intact and terror states unchecked—our sense of security would be false and temporary.[23]

After outlining the depth and breadth of the threat, the speaker then discussed homeland security and linked terrorism, with its related issues, to domestic issues, such as crime and public safety services, and brought the threat down to the level of the individual. Instead of distancing Americans from difficult foreign policy issues such as North Korea and nuclear proliferation, the speaker thereby tried to make the expanding terrorism issue more relevant to the citizen, implying a civic responsibility to deal with the growing problem:

> Homeland security will make America not only stronger, but, in many ways, better. Knowledge gained from bioterrorism research will improve public health. Stronger police and fire departments will mean safer neighborhoods. Stricter border enforcement will help combat illegal drugs. (Applause.) And as government works to better secure our homeland, America will continue to depend on the eyes and ears of alert citizens.[24]

> Members, you and I will work together in the months ahead on other issues: productive farm policy—(applause)—a cleaner environment—(applause)—broader home ownership, especially among minorities—(applause)—and ways to encourage the

good work of charities and faith-based groups. (Applause.) I ask you to join me on these important domestic issues in the same spirit of cooperation we've applied to our war against terrorism.[25]

Once we have funded our national security and our homeland security, the final great priority of my budget is economic security for the American people.[26]

By tying future losses to domestic issues, Bush brought foreign policy and budget issues together under the economic security concept at the same time the United States was facing an economic recession. Since financing the war on terror and military operations abroad would require significant spending, this was an effective framing proposal if Bush was able to establish that the U.S. security arena was at a loss. By bringing the problem to the individual level, this was an effective agenda-setting approach in the sense that it mixed domestic budgetary issues with foreign policy issues that were typically out of the domestic policy realm.

Although it is too early in the timeframe to show direct causal links, it is possible to outline the various types of framing and their consistency when leading up to policy decisions. Loss framing within the State of the Union Address focused on showing the terrorist threat as being greater and more widespread than the September 11 attacks, as well as linking potential losses from terrorism with other foreign policy issues. Although this single speech did not result in greater leadership approval for the president, it framed terrorism as a broad issue on different levels. It rested the burden of responsibility on the individual citizen while linking the individual to a variety of foreign policy issues. The speaker's ability to play on the atmosphere of vulnerability to such an attentive audience gave the loss framing increased salience and connected foreign policy with domestic policy issues through thematic framing. By the time the Iraq war began, a significant percentage of Americans not only believed that terrorism was a major threat to their safety but also linked the war in Iraq with the broader U.S. war on terrorism.[27]

FRAMING IRAQ

Early in 2002, the president introduced new thematic framing on Iraq and attempted to combine separate policy streams by linking Iraq and terrorism into a more interconnected issue. Interestingly, as the war on terror theme became more salient to the public, Bush introduced economic security as a policy stream by linking the economy with the war on terror. With respect to the various types of framing effects in this chapter, attention will focus on the chronology of the loss framing as it is the cornerstone of policy rhetoric leading up to the war in Iraq.

In framing Iraq, the president used a pattern of communication similar to his introductions on the U.S. war on terror and U.S. missions in Afghanistan. He reiterated a picture of threats to the United States and continued with that message until the execution of the policy. While frequency levels were low until September, hovering below ten instances per month throughout early 2002, framing Iraq as a threat defined the policy debate by the time it peaked in the fall of 2002. Mentions of the Iraq threat typically fit the thematic frame established during the State of the Union Address.

Therefore, while Iraq was mentioned relatively infrequently in early 2002, the frequency of its mention and related framing increased and peaked at 120 instances in October while the president pushed for support of the Iraq Resolution and made a similar argument in front of the United Nations. After policy implementation, the administration relied on his previous framing of the issue to justify policy changes. Overall, this provided a continuous message to guide the public in how to define the policy debate.

At the time of the State of the Union Address, most Americans were not convinced that Iraq represented a clear and imminent danger to the United States. However, Americans' views on Iraq as a hostile regime had shifted over time and that view was pliable. The State of the Union Address provided an opportunity to set the tone for America's policy on Iraq. By the time Bush made the push to pass the Iraq Resolution, Americans' views had begun to shift toward accepting a risky policy change. Thus it was important to introduce a thematic frame about Iraq that would continue over time and allow the president to push forth clear and simple threat rhetoric. The excerpts below highlight the framing of the Iraq issue. These frames continued through the fall of 2002, when Bush achieved significant support for his stance on Iraq. The public accepted his definition of the policy debate and saw Iraq as a threat to U.S. security.

In the State of the Union Address, Bush linked Iraq with the broader and more salient terrorism issue. This included discussion of WMDs, which both Bush and Powell later highlighted when arguing similar Iraq framing to the United Nations. Here, the theme underscored Iraq's support for terrorism and its history of WMDs use. These consistent thematic frames regarding Iraq and WMDs as threats to U.S. security defined the foreign policy debate for the Bush administration and set the groundwork for outlining future foreign policy choices to the public. Tracking the thematic frames over time, it is possible to see how framing that was introduced in January 2002 was used at key points in time, resulting in relatively successful public opinion rallies at key policy junctures (Figure 5.1).

President Bush introduced new themes into the foreign policy message in the State of The Union Address. With respect to framing, the speech provided a significant political communication platform since speech content and audience turnout were both factors in the importance of this particular address. The following excerpts from the State of the Union Address highlight the consistency of thematic framing in introducing the Iraq issue to the public:

Iraq continues to flaunt its hostility toward America and to support terror. The Iraqi regime has plotted to develop anthrax, and nerve gas, and nuclear weapons for over a decade. This is a regime that has already used poison gas to murder thousands of its own citizens—leaving the bodies of mothers huddled over their dead children. This is

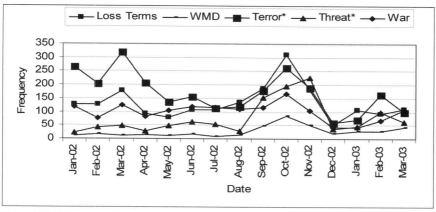

Figure 5.1   Thematic Framing and Loss Domain Terms

a regime that agreed to international inspections—then kicked out the inspectors. This is a regime that has something to hide from the civilized world. States like these, and their terrorist allies, constitute an axis of evil, arming to threaten the peace of the world. By seeking weapons of mass destruction, these regimes pose a grave and growing danger. They could provide these arms to terrorists, giving them the means to match their hatred. They could attack our allies or attempt to blackmail the United States. In any of these cases, the price of indifference would be catastrophic.[28]

We'll be deliberate, yet time is not on our side. I will not wait on events, while dangers gather. I will not stand by, as peril draws closer and closer. The United States of America will not permit the world's most dangerous regimes to threaten us with the world's most destructive weapons.[29]

Bush introduced Iraq as a state that possessed WMDs and used them on a civilian population. On the UN inspections issue, Bush introduced Iraq as an untrustworthy state that hid its internal affairs from the international community. Last, he offered the connection between Iraq's WMDs program and terrorism. Again, the time-sensitive element was introduced, highlighting the potential for loss. The overall loss and thematic framing of the Iraq issue presented an inherently limited set of policy choices. Observing that the status quo presented a loss left many opportunities to introduce more risky policy options.

LOSS DOMAIN TERMS

Loss domain frequencies were low and steady for the first seven months of 2002. March showed greater discussion of the terror theme, which rose significantly but did not affect Bush's leadership ratings (Figure 5.1). This would also have little effect on terrorism's salience to the public, which already viewed potential terrorist attacks as the main threat to U.S. security. Some of the March peak can also be attributed to references to the death tax issue and other references point to the March 12 release of the national color-coded advisory system. Loss domain rhetoric was focused on WMDs and defeating the enemy. At the beginning of the year, Bush's message focused mostly on preventing terrorism and the new status quo of America's war on terrorism. There were continuous references to those that wear the uniform, nations and terrorists that want to harm the United States, and terrorists and nations with access to WMDs. Discussion of al-Qaeda, as well as other, vaguer enemies, became the new background noise of political rhetoric.

> And we're making good progress, and I appreciate the resolve and patience of our country. I appreciate the unity that stands behind the men and women who wear our uniform.[30]

> This nation will not tire, we will not rest until we bring those who are willing to harm Americans to justice. And that's exactly what we intend to do.[31]

> We understand the importance of denying terrorists weapons of mass destruction. And we understand the importance of adapting NATO to meet new threats, even as NATO prepares to take on new members and forges a new relationship with Russia.[32]

While mentions of terrorism and WMDs became consistently present in Bush's public speeches, the earlier speeches for 2002 shed light on the type of loss domain rhetoric and framing that will be seen during the build-up period. Consistency between large increases in frequency levels and public rallying effects will be examined next, as well as causal linkage between the presidential approval polls, support for war, and presidential policy decisions.

BUILD-UP

The build-up period covers August through November 2002. In this timeframe, we will see large changes in framing and rhetoric, followed by notable changes in public opinion on (1) presidential leadership, (2) support for military action against Iraq, and (3) whether Iraq was a threat to the United States. During this timeframe, the president initiated his persuasion of Congress to support the Iraq Resolution. In addition to utilizing framing and rhetoric similar to his marketing of the Afghanistan policy, Bush used the first anniversary of the September 11 attacks to rally public opinion in support of his preemptive strategy on Iraq.

The first changes to be noticed were in the loss domain frequency category, which rose in September and peaked in October (Figure 5.1). The following excerpts from various speeches indicate that loss domain rhetoric focused on previous themes such as the September 11 attacks, the protection of the United States from further harm, and America's new vulnerability:

> On September the 11th we'll mourn the **loss** of life, we'll remember what happened to us.[33]

> And so long as we hold these values dear, which we will do, there will be an enemy trying to **hurt** America. And so, therefore, my most important job is to protect the American people from further **harm**, is to guard our homeland.[34]

> We used to think, well, there's a little conflict going over there, or perhaps a leader over here who is a despicable person couldn't **hurt** us. We learned a new lesson after September the 11th, that we're vulnerable.[35]

OVERALL FRAMING

The overall frequency of framing and rhetoric indicated that Bush's marketing campaign peaked in October, less than six months prior to the U.S.-led invasion of Iraq. The various types of framing linked Iraq to terrorism and presented it as a future WMDs/terrorist threat to the United States. Threat framing was presented along similar lines and linked Iraq to WMDs and terrorism. In October, the major thematic frames, terror, WMDs, threat, war, as well as loss domain rhetoric, converged to clearly define Iraq as a threat to U.S. security (Figure 5.2).

This was the president's rhetorical push to convince Congress and the American public that Iraq was a threat and that maintaining status quo would lead the United States to future losses. The following excerpts are taken from a sample of speeches

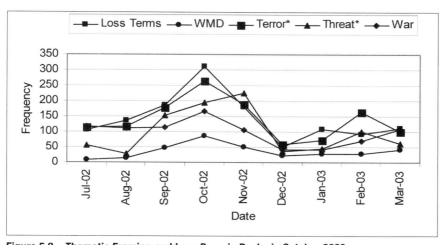

Figure 5.2   Thematic Framing and Loss Domain Peaks in October 2002

given in September and October and represent the variety of framing effects during those months. The speeches define the threat, link Iraq with WMDs, and point to risky policy options while rejecting the status quo. According to public opinion polls, the terror and WMDs frames were most effective in defining Iraq as a threat:

> Yesterday I announced to the country that I would be working closely with our United States Congress and the American people to explain the **threat** that Saddam Hussein poses to world peace. I take the **threat** very seriously. I take the fact that he develops **weapons of mass destruction** very seriously.[36]

> We can't look at the world the way we hope the world would be. We must look at the world the way it is. We must see **threats** for what they are. And there's a true **threat** to America and our friends and allies in Iraq. Saddam Hussein—Saddam Hussein is a man who told the world that he would have no **weapons of mass destruction**. He deceived the world.[37]

> But let me say to you that the issue is not inspectors, the issue is disarmament. This is a man who said he would not arm up. This is a man who told the world that he would not harbor **weapons of mass destruction**. That's the primary issue. And I'll be discussing ways to make sure that that is the case.[38]

> This man is a man who said he was going to get rid of **weapons of mass destruction**. And for 11 long years, he has not fulfilled his promise. And we're going to talk about what to do about it. We owe it to future generations to deal with this problem, and that's what these discussions are all about.[39]

The October 7 address to the nation, outlining the Iraqi threat, was a key foreign policy speech prior to the Senate's bipartisan approval of the Iraq Resolution. The final vote was seventy-seven to twenty-three. The following sections outline the variety of Bush's framing on Iraq. While the intention here is to systematically categorize the various frames of loss, threat, and terror, many of the excerpts contain a crossover of different frames.

LOSS FRAMING

These examples of loss framing illustrate how the president was trying to convince the public and Congress to take a gamble in order to avoid future losses. They focused on Iraq's growing strength, the development of more WMDs, the development of WMD delivery systems to strike the United States and its allies, and the likelihood that Iraq would provide terrorists with WMD capabilities:

> Some ask how urgent this danger is to America and the world. The danger is already significant, and it only grows worse with time. If we know Saddam Hussein has dangerous weapons today—and we do—does it make any sense for the world to wait to confront him as he grows even stronger and develops even more dangerous weapons.[40]

Iraq possesses ballistic missiles with a likely range of hundreds of miles—far enough to strike Saudi Arabia, Israel, Turkey, and other nations—in a region where more than 135,000 American civilians and service members live and work. We've also discovered through intelligence that Iraq has a growing fleet of manned and unmanned aerial vehicles that could be used to disperse chemical or biological weapons across broad areas. We're concerned that Iraq is exploring ways of using these UAVS for missions targeting the United States. And, of course, sophisticated delivery systems aren't required for a chemical or biological attack; all that might be required are a small container and one terrorist or Iraqi intelligence operative to deliver it.[41]

Iraq could decide on any given day to provide a biological or chemical weapon to a terrorist group or individual terrorists. Alliance with terrorists could allow the Iraqi regime to attack America without leaving any fingerprints.

Some have argued that confronting the threat from Iraq could detract from the war against terror. To the contrary; confronting the threat posed by Iraq is crucial to winning the war on terror. When I spoke to Congress more than a year ago, I said that those who harbor terrorists are as guilty as the terrorists themselves. Saddam Hussein is harboring terrorists and the instruments of terror, the instruments of mass death and destruction. And he cannot be trusted. The risk is simply too great that he will use them, or provide them to a terror network.[42]

If the Iraqi regime is able to produce, buy or steal an amount of highly enriched uranium a little larger than a single softball, it could have a nuclear weapon in less than a year. And if we allow that to happen, a terrible line would be crossed. Saddam Hussein would be in a position to blackmail anyone who opposes his aggression. He would be in a position to dominate the Middle East. He would be in a position to threaten America. And Saddam Hussein would be in a position to pass nuclear technology to terrorists.[43]

Here, the speaker reiterated the growing threat and argued that maintaining the status quo in order to gain more evidence could lead to even greater losses:

Knowing these realities, America must not ignore the threat gathering against us. Facing clear evidence of peril, we cannot wait for the final proof—the smoking gun—that could come in the form of a mushroom cloud.[44]

Failure to act would embolden other tyrants, allow terrorists access to new weapons and new resources, and make blackmail a permanent feature of world events. The United Nations would betray the purpose of its founding, and prove irrelevant to the problems of our time. And through its inaction, the United States would resign itself to a future of fear.[45]

Understanding the threats of our time, knowing the designs and deceptions of the Iraqi regime, we have every reason to assume the worst, and we have an urgent duty to prevent the worst from occurring.[46]

The attacks of September the 11th showed our country that vast oceans no longer protect us from danger. Before that tragic date, we had only hints of al Qaeda's plans and designs. Today in Iraq, we see a threat whose outlines are far more clearly defined, and whose consequences could be far more deadly. Saddam Hussein's actions have put us on notice, and there is no refuge from our responsibilities.[47]

THREAT FRAMING

In using threat framing, the president used threat rhetoric to define Iraq as a threat to the United States and to the status quo. He utilized historical references and Iraq's links to terrorism and WMD proliferation in defining the theme:

> Tonight I want to take a few minutes to discuss a grave **threat** to peace, and America's determination to lead the world in confronting that **threat**. The **threat** comes from Iraq. It arises directly from the Iraqi regime's own actions—its history of aggression, and its drive toward an arsenal of terror.[48]

> Members of the Congress of both political parties, and members of the United Nations Security Council, agree that Saddam Hussein is a **threat** to peace and must disarm. We agree that the Iraqi dictator must not be permitted to **threaten** America and the world with horrible poisons and diseases and gases and atomic weapons.[49]

> We also must never forget the most vivid events of recent history. On September the 11th, 2001, America felt its vulnerability—even to **threats** that gather on the other side of the earth. We resolved then, and we are resolved today, to confront every **threat**, from any source, that could bring sudden terror and suffering to America.[50]

TERROR FRAMING

The terror frame was effective in promoting the theme to the American people. It represents one of the sides of the triangle of effective thematic framing: terror, WMDs, and threat rhetoric. The following excerpts show how Bush defined the debate on Iraq by linking it with what the public considered as the main threat to U.S. security—terrorism.

> We know that the regime has produced thousands of tons of chemical agents, including mustard gas, sarin nerve gas, VX nerve gas. Saddam Hussein also has experience in using chemical weapons. He has ordered chemical attacks on Iran, and on more than forty villages in his own country. These actions killed or injured at least 20,000 people, more than six times the number of people who died in the attacks of September the 11th.[51]

> The Iraqi regime has violated all of those obligations. It possesses and produces chemical and biological weapons. It is seeking nuclear weapons. It has given shelter and support to **terrorism**, and practices **terror** against its own people. The entire world has witnessed Iraq's eleven-year history of defiance, deception and bad faith.[52]

And that is the source of our urgent concern about Saddam Hussein's links to international **terrorist** groups. Over the years, Iraq has provided safe haven to **terrorists** such as Abu Nidal, whose **terror** organization carried out more than 90 **terrorist** attacks in 20 countries that killed or injured nearly 900 people, including 12 Americans. Iraq has also provided safe haven to Abu Abbas, who was responsible for seizing the Achille Lauro and killing an American passenger. And we know that Iraq is continuing to finance **terror** and gives assistance to groups that use **terrorism** to undermine Middle East peace.[53]

We know that Iraq and the al Qaeda **terrorist** network share a common enemy—the United States of America. We know that Iraq and al Qaeda have had high-level contacts that go back a decade. Some al Qaeda leaders who fled Afghanistan went to Iraq. These include one very senior al Qaeda leader who received medical treatment in Baghdad this year, and who has been associated with planning for chemical and biological attacks. We've learned that Iraq has trained al Qaeda members in bomb-making and poisons and deadly gases. And we know that after September the 11th, Saddam Hussein's regime gleefully celebrated the **terrorist** attacks on America.[54]

OUTLINING POLICY OPTIONS

Part of prospect theory research focuses on how an actor outlines policy options for the audience. Some of this research looks at how advisors presented policy options to the decision maker. In this case, the president outlined policy options for the public and discounted the pursuit of the status quo. In general, he presented the option of escalated military action as the best way to avoid future losses:

Some believe we can address this danger by simply resuming the old approach to inspections, and applying diplomatic and economic pressure. Yet this is precisely what the world has tried to do since 1991. The U.N. inspections program was met with systematic deception.[55]

The world has also tried economic sanctions—and watched Iraq use billions of dollars in illegal oil revenues to fund more weapons purchases, rather than providing for the needs of the Iraqi people.[56]

Here the president listed limited military strikes as part of the status quo, leaving escalation as a policy option to avoid future losses:

The world has tried limited military strikes to destroy Iraq's weapons of mass destruction capabilities—only to see them openly rebuilt, while the regime again denies they even exist. The world has tried no-fly zones to keep Saddam from terrorizing his own people—and in the last year alone, the Iraqi military has fired upon American and British pilots more than 750 times.[57]

After eleven years during which we have tried containment, sanctions, inspections, even selected military action, the end result is that Saddam Hussein still has chemical and biological weapons and is increasing his capabilities to make more. And he is moving ever closer to developing a nuclear weapon.[58]

A contradictory policy option is presented here, offering to improve status quo policies without military escalation:

> Clearly, to actually work, any new inspections, sanctions or enforcement mechanisms will have to be very different. America wants the U.N. to be an effective organization that helps keep the peace. And that is why we are urging the Security Council to adopt a new resolution setting out tough, immediate requirements. Among those requirements: the Iraqi regime must reveal and destroy, under U.N. supervision, all existing weapons of mass destruction. To ensure that we learn the truth, the regime must allow witnesses to its illegal activities to be interviewed outside the country—and these witnesses must be free to bring their families with them so they all beyond the reach of Saddam Hussein's terror and murder. And inspectors must have access to any site, at any time, without pre-clearance, without delay, without exceptions.[59]

Toward the end of the October 7 speech, the president again discounted the status quo as a loss and frames immediate action as a way to avoid future losses: "There is no easy or risk-free course of action. Some have argued we should wait—and that's an option. In my view, it's the riskiest of all options, because the longer we wait, the stronger and bolder Saddam Hussein will become."[60]

While the president was effective in convincing Congress and the American people that Iraq was a threat to the United States, not everyone was convinced that he had a clear plan. Therefore, while the variety of framing and rhetoric defined the debate for the public, a lack of clear a clear Iraq strategy was also noted in public polling data.[61]

GAIN AND THEMATIC FRAMING

While a cost-benefit calculation would prescribe that the American public needs to perceive success or progress in order to continue to pay the costs, the data showed that Bush's speeches continued to focus mostly on discussing losses and the now growing war on terror (Table 5.1).

When compared to loss framing, presidential cheerleading of future gains did not occur to a significant degree, nor did it show a strong association to changes in public opinion polls.

PUBLIC OPINION

Mention of Iraq and relevant framing peaked in October 2002, the same month the Iraq Resolution was passed by Congress with bipartisan support. During the same period, Bush's leadership indexes rose approximately 10 percentage points between

Table 5.1 Thematic Framing Data

Date	Loss Domain Terms	Terror	Threat	Victory	Win
Jan-02	128	265	22	7	36
Feb-02	126	203	42	3	10
Mar-02	179	318	47	9	25
Apr-02	94	207	28	6	10
May-02	79	136	47	14	15
Jun-02	106	155	62	6	19
Jul-02	106	113	55	5	29
Aug-02	**135**	**118**	29	4	33
Sep-02	**186**	**178**	**152**	2	14
Oct-02	**310**	**263**	**194**	0	**39**
Nov-02	**181**	**190**	**225**	4	20
Dec-02	50	58	37	3	8
Jan-03	108	71	44	2	9
Feb-03	92	164	100	2	10
Mar-03	110	99	61	18	11

September and December, depending on index.[62] Consequently, Americans' acceptance of Iraq as having high-level ties to al-Qaeda and possessing WMDs was on the increase. Bush's framing of the Iraq/terrorism/WMD issue was gaining resonance with the American public.

Part of the explanation for this increase in the leadership index is linked with Bush's increase in war rhetoric, which peaked a month after the first anniversary of September 11. This created a historical but short rally around the flag effect. The timing of the push to pass the Iraq Resolution and the increase in war rhetoric coincided with the September 11 anniversary to a loose degree, and those variables coming together in that time period likely played a role in increasing the president's leadership index.

In September and November, 64 percent of Americans supported military action in Iraq, according to an ABC news poll. According to the Pew Research Center, 62 percent of Americans supported military action against Iraq, while only 28 percent opposed such action. The majority that supported military action cited the Iraq/terrorism connection as a threat to U.S. security.[63] However, the slight rise in support for use of military force lasted beyond Bush's war rhetoric peaks. According to an ABC news poll, when respondents were asked, "Would you favor or oppose having U.S. forces take military action against Iraq to force Saddam Hussein from power?" a clear majority maintained support leading up to the March 2003 invasion.[64] Furthermore, when asked if they viewed Iraq as a threat to the United States, the number of respondents answering yes peaked at 81 percent from December 2002 through January 2003.[65] Although this is a small rise in the range of support, it nevertheless increased after Bush's rhetorical push with Congress and the public for military intervention with Iraq.

The president's message that Iraq was a threat because of its relation to the WMDs/terrorism issue resonated extremely well with the public. When asked if disarming Iraq while leaving Saddam Hussein in power was adequate versus removing Hussein from power, 85 percent responded that Iraq's leader needed to be removed.[66] Unexpectedly, 70 percent of both supporters and opponents of military action agreed that Iraq posed a threat to the United States. In early October, even before Bush's October 7 speech making the case for military action against Iraq, the American public was listening and accepting Bush's risk communication on the issue. Seventy percent of the public believed that Iraq already possessed WMDs, and two-thirds believed that Saddam Hussein had a role in the September 11 attacks.

This means that some type of effect from Bush's speech framing carried over beyond the rhetoric peak in October. The public and the media were receptive to different thematic frames at different rates. While support for the president did not experience a large jump, the public became more aware of the president's message. The consistency and timing of the rhetoric altered how those communications entered the public's consciousness and defined the debate, resulting in scattered public opinion results. However, it is important that support for military action was increasing while no exogenous events occurred to produce a rally around the flag effect. The anniversary of the September 11 attacks a month before the rhetoric frequency peak certainly may have contributed to a rise in support for military action, however, the September 11 anniversary cannot alone account for an increase in public recognition of Iraq as a threat; this means that events such as terrorist attacks against the United States or the president initiating attacks against Iraq were absent and could not have produced a rally around the flag effect. The lack of traditional rallying events points to variance in Bush's war rhetoric as an explanatory variable for increases in public support.

One effect that may also account for the public's awareness of the WMDs/Iraq issue is the media's magnification of certain themes and frames, which may account for why the WMDs theme did not show frequency results as high as the terror and threat theme content analysis. However, polling data showed significant public salience regarding the Iraq/terrorism/WMDs issue. In September, 79 percent of the public believed that Iraq already had the ability to strike targets within the United States with WMDs.[67] However, at that time, most Americans still did not see Iraq as much of a threat to U.S. security as al-Qaeda when asked to rank most urgent foreign policy problems. Consequently, successfully establishing an Iraq/terrorism link was vital to gaining greater support for long-term military action against Iraq.

While the White House should be considered a significant agenda setter on foreign policy issues, the media also played a large role in promoting the administration's Iraq agenda. In looking at the media's role in promoting the Bush administration's message, there are a number of issues raised by scholars regarding magnifying war rhetoric and framing effects. Some of those criticisms relate to the media's close relationship to the White House, the media's technologically inaccurate coverage of the WMDs issue, and the media's complicity in promoting the Iraq/terrorism/WMDs connection without critical analysis.

Intervening variables aside, an interesting dual effect was unfolding in the public opinion data. While public support for military intervention was increasing, this support was not wholehearted, and the nature of this duality can help explain the decrease in war support a year after the March 2003 invasion.

While Americans overwhelmingly supported disarming and removing Saddam Hussein, there was decrease in support for military action among Americans identifying themselves as having thought a lot about the issue. Furthermore, a 56 percent majority stated that there was still a chance to avoid war with Iraq altogether.[68] These results show some contradictory information. While a majority of Americans saw Iraq as a threat and supported military action to oust Saddam Hussein from power, their support showed some weakening when asked about how willing they were to support a long-term war with significant casualties. Furthermore, a third believed that the president was rushing to war.

After follow-up questions, a majority of Americans continued to support military action against Iraq, but there was a decrease in support. This is indicative of war rhetoric that is not fully penetrating the audience. Although Bush's Iraq message seemed to be getting across, Americans' support for war showed signs of weakening when questioned about how support would vary depending upon levels of U.S. casualties, allied support, and whether invading Iraq will aid in fighting the war on terror. Although even after these qualifiers, overall support for military action was a majority, the fact that support deceased in the face of potential problems with the war was indicative of the public's limited understanding of what a war in Iraq could require.

Furthermore, since this weakening of support occurred during the height of Bush's push for war, it would be fair to speculate that a percentage of American support for war was for reasons other than Iraq being a threat. September 11 background conditions likely played a role in Americans' support, or it may be that the president's framing of the threat was effective because of the WMDs issue, without which support for the war weakened. Put more simply, the public had just supported the president to such a high degree that they were more than willing to listen to his framing of the issue, bypassing critical analysis. Therefore, in the post–September 11 atmosphere, it was possible for the president to market risk more effectively than prior to the attacks.

IRAQ INVASION

The pre-invasion rhetoric results outline the lack of sufficient marketing to sell a preemptive war against Iraq. During this period, the results showed no rise in loss domain rhetoric, only a slight rise in the terror theme and no frequency increases in the relevant thematic frames (Figure 5.1). The majority of the foreign policy selling occurred during the fall of 2002. Meanwhile, polling conducted in February

2002 showed that 66 percent of the public supported military action against Iraq only with adequate international backing. However, 56 percent of the public believed that the United States did not have enough international backing at the time.[69] Yet the president was doing little else to garner more public support for the war. Most of his rhetoric focused on the terror theme, including references to the September 11 attacks:

> The Secretary of State has now briefed the United Nations Security Council on Iraq's illegal weapons programs, its attempts to hide those weapons, and its links to **terrorist** groups.[70]

> Saddam Hussein has long-standing, direct and continuing ties to **terrorist** networks. Senior members of Iraqi intelligence and al Qaeda have met at least eight times since the early 1990s. Iraq has sent bomb-making and document forgery experts to work with al Qaeda. Iraq has also provided al Qaeda with chemical and biological weapons training.[71]

> A regime that aids and harbors **terrorists** and is armed with weapons of mass murder. Before September the 11th, 2001, there's a lot of good folks who believe that Saddam Hussein can be contained. Before September the 11th, 2001, we thought oceans would protect us forever; that if we saw a gathering threat somewhere else in the world, we could respond to it if we chose—so chose to do so. But that all changed on that fateful day. Chemical agents, lethal viruses and shadowy **terrorist** networks are not easily contained.[72]

> We also know that Iraq is harboring a **terrorist** network, headed by a senior al Qaeda terrorist planner.[73]

> This war requires us to understand that **terror** is broader than one international network, that these **terrorist** networks have got connections—in some cases, to countries run by outlaw dictators. And that's the issue with Iraq. When I speak about the war on **terror**, I not only talk about al Qaeda, I talk about Iraq—because, after all, Saddam Hussein has got weapons of mass destruction and he's used them.[74]

> Saddam Hussein is used to deceiving the world and he continues to do so. Saddam Hussein has got ties to **terrorist** networks.[75]

> The same **terrorist** network operating out of Iraq is responsible for the murder, the recent murder, of an American citizen, an American diplomat, Laurence Foley. The same network has plotted **terrorism** against France, Spain, Italy, Germany, the Republic of Georgia and Russia, and was caught producing poisons in London. The danger Saddam Hussein poses reaches across the world.[76]

> We will not wait to see what **terrorists** or **terrorist** states could do with chemical, biological, radiological or nuclear weapons. Saddam Hussein can now be expected to begin another round of empty concessions, transparently false denials. No doubt, he will play a last-minute game of deception. The game is over.[77]

In our country it used to be that oceans could protect us—at least we thought so. There was wars on other continents, but we were safe. And so we could decide whether or not we addressed the threat on our own time. If there was a threat gathering from afar, we could say, well, let's see, it may be in our interest to get involved, or it may not be. We had the luxury. September the 11th, that changed. America is now a battleground in the war on **terror**.[78]

I worry about a future in which Saddam Hussein gets to blackmail and/or attack. I worry about a future in which **terrorist** organizations are fueled and funded by a Saddam Hussein. And that's why we're bringing this issue to a head.[79]

This same tyrant has close ties to **terrorist** organizations, and could supply them with the terrible means to strike this country—and America will not permit it. The danger posed by Saddam Hussein and his weapons cannot be ignored or wished away. The danger must be confronted. We hope that the Iraqi regime will meet the demands of the United Nations and disarm, fully and peacefully. If it does not, we are prepared to disarm Iraq by force.[80]

The immediate pre-invasion picture showed a presidential marketing campaign that fell short of fully persuading the American public to go to war without sufficient international support. While the president did an outstanding job of convincing the public that Iraq had terrorist connections and possessed WMDs that could be used to arm al-Qaeda terrorists, he failed to garner enough support for the United States to pursue a preemptive war with less than full multilateral support.[81] Nevertheless, with limited framing and rhetoric supporting the war on the eve of the U.S.-led invasion, the president experienced a 15 percent boost in leadership ratings in some polling data, likely resulting from a rally around the flag effect.[82] The rally around the flag effect generated support for military action at slightly higher levels than during the president's peak war framing period in October.[83]

CONCLUSION

In the long term, framing that was effective in promoting support for punitive war in Afghanistan was not quite as effective in promoting support for preemptive war in Iraq. However, short-term linkages appear to have potential for further research. Usage of thematic framing along with loss domain terms in public speeches does connect well with shifting public opinion. According to the polling data, Bush's war rhetoric on Iraq was successful in framing Iraq as a threat to U.S. security, but not successful enough to win support for a less than fully multilateral war effort.[84] The lack of long-term support can be attributed to weak marketing efforts immediately prior to the invasion, the lack of clear evidence linking Iraq to al-Qaeda and current WMDs production, or a mix of the two.

However, this is a tautological argument. If the president had clear evidence of Iraq's WMDs possession, then he may not have needed such pervasive and ubiquitous war framing. It is possible to argue that precisely because of the elusive smoking gun evidence, the president needed to rely on his ability to frame a potential threat for the public. This investigation is not about the validity of the president's argument but about his choice of rhetorical tools. While the mere existence of the president's war framing does not establish causality, shifts in the public's support for war while lacking clear evidence of a newly emerging and growing threat support an argument for framing as playing some type of role, albeit indirect, in shifting the public's domain and increasing support for a risky foreign policy change. By looking at whether gain frames helped in maintaining risky war policy, it will be possible to see if the public was willing to maintain costs when faced with future gains.

The next chapter will show that the president did not adequately convince the public that future losses would be greater than present costs. According to prospect theory, in order to convince an audience to accept costly options, the audience must believe that they are doing so to avoid even greater costs in the long run. Apparently, prior to the Iraq War, the public bought into the "either we fight the enemy there or we'll be fighting them on the streets of America" argument enough for the president to implement war policy without full multilateral support. This is critical because as the next chapter will show, it becomes extremely difficult to convince the public to accept further costs when it appears that there are no more losses left to avoid. Thus, once a state is actively engaged in war, if the previously advertised losses such as the Iraq/terrorism/WMDs links fail to materialize, then there may not be enough of a potential threat that is convincing enough for the public to continue to accept growing costs.

The president's recent strategy document, the National Strategy for Victory in Iraq, highlights future gains for Iraq as well as an avoidance of losses in the form of increased terrorism.[85] This strategy runs counter to prospect theory tenets in the sense that it is asking people to continue accepting costs while working toward greater gains. If framing gains for Iraq translate into increased support for the war in Iraq, then prospect theory's outline of framing effects may require reevaluation. However, the evidence in this case supports the prospect theory form of framing as opposed to the cost-benefit approach to framing.

Recent research attempts posit that the public may be willing to continue accepting costs if the goal is clear and winnable.[86] However, this implies that actors who were willing to pay costs in order to avoid losses would now agree to continue paying costs to make future gains. That type of logic falls back on a cost-benefit calculation but fails to show adequate representation in the president's communication on the war in Iraq.

The War on Terror in Iraq

DURING THE OCCUPATION and rebuilding stage of the Iraq war, President Bush used thematic framing, specifically the terror frame that had been related to identifying future losses, to boost diminishing support for the war and ultimately support for himself during an election year. By further reinforcing the idea that the war in Iraq was part of the broader war on terrorism, he effectively garnered just enough war support to gain a slight majority while winning the 2004 elections. Bush's execution of the postinvasion marketing campaign constituted a repackaging of his pre–Iraq invasion rhetoric with a greater focus on the war on terror theme. Essentially, this was Bush's previous war rhetoric in a leaner and more focused format in which the Iraq war became part of the war on terror.

Bush's earlier framing of the war on terror was linked to previous and future losses. The frame itself was effective in establishing and maintaining the policy debate so that additional themes were not required. For the president and for a majority of the American people, the United States was at war with terrorism and the battle was now being fought on the streets of Baghdad, Fallujah, and Tikrit. As the data will show, the American public perceived three vital issues: (1) at some point in time, Iraq pursued a WMDs program, (2) Iraq had some type of links to al-Qaeda, and (3) America's priority was to fight the war on terror. Through effective framing, Bush created long-lasting issue saliency in the public's awareness. The war on terror provided a nearly unattainable goal in prospect theory terms; it was an aspiration level that continued to place the American public in the domain of loss and willing to expend the necessary costs.

During the occupation and rebuilding of Iraq, Bush brought the war on terror back into focus. Meanwhile, Iraq's unfolding insurgency helped support the perception that the United States was now fighting the war on terror against radical extremists streaming into Iraq. With the media's focus on Iraq's unexpected insurgency, the president simply needed to reassert the policy debate and point out that America's war on terror was now taking place in Iraq as well as Afghanistan. As the president frequently pointed out, fighting the war on terror in Iraq was always better than fighting it on the streets of America.

The record high usage of terror framing is interconnected with increases in public support at critical junctures for the president and his foreign policy. During that time, thematic framing of victory, winning, and success in Iraq showed only slight increases in frequency. While discussion of winning and victories in the war on terror were present, the overwhelming majority of the president's framing focused on the threat of terrorism. In a somewhat intangible way, the president's rhetoric was greater than the sum of its parts as it created greater meaning and saliency for the public. In fact, a segment of the population tended to believe the president simply because of his position. As a consequence, the president's framing carried additional weight as a result of its source.

President Bush's framing alone was not responsible for his successful reelection campaign, but the argument presented here is that presidential framing played a major role in achieving that goal. This chapter continues to pursue the underlining argument that the public acts as a short-term security maximizer that discounts long-term benefits, inflates near-term threats, and is perceptive to national security framing. Following that line of logic, the president's rhetoric continued to focus on the costs of a terrorist threat rather than the limited gains made in Iraq. While both forms of framing existed, the former dominated Bush's rhetoric.

The timeframe for this chapter begins in May 2003 and ends in December 2004, after the president's successful reelection campaign. This timeframe covers two main events correlating to changes between presidential framing, rhetoric, and changes in public support: first, the 1000-casualty milestone suffered by U.S. forces in Iraq; second, the dramatic framing changes leading up to the 2004 election, followed by slight changes in public support for the war and the president.

THE CASUALTY MILESTONE

In June 2003, support for the war in Iraq continued to remain strong at 68 percent and 74 percent of the public agreed that Bush was showing strong leadership skills.[1] At the same time, an increasing majority of the public grew skeptical of the Iraq-terrorism–September 11 attacks link previously presented by the Bush administration. The data showed an interesting dichotomy in the results: while people did not necessarily agree that going to war in Iraq was the right decision if the WMDs and terrorism link was false, they still supported Bush's decision because of his position as president.[2] Public support for the war in Iraq began to decrease in the summer of 2003 and dipped in September when the U.S. casualty count reached the 1000 mark.[3]

With the milestone widely reported by the media, the president's approval and support for war ratings dipped but then recovered. The TIPP Presidential Index fell from 66.2 to 63.3 in October, and then rose to 65 in November.[4] A CNN, *USA Today*, and Gallup poll asking, "All in all, do you think it was worth going to war in Iraq, or not?" showed a decrease from 63 to 50 percent in support in September, then rose to 59 percent in December, prior to Saddam Hussein's capture.[5] A Pew survey asking, "Do you think the U.S. made the right decision or the wrong decision in using military force against Iraq?" showed a low of 60 percent war support in October, immediately after the casualty milestone, but then rose to 69 percent after the president's push to regain support despite mounting casualties. At the same time, we witnessed the first noticeable peak in presidential terror framing since the U.S. invasion of Iraq. While throughout the first half of 2003, the terror frame occurred approximately 200 instances per month, the frequency jumped to 400 instances following the media's reporting of the casualty milestone.

The peak in terror framing was likely a reaction to the U.S. casualty milestone. Bush's immediate rallying attempts were followed by a moderate recovery in support for war, as measured by a variety of polling data. This recovery took place prior to Saddam Hussein's capture, which contributed to another rise in ratings. This tells us that aside from exogenous events such as progress in the war, the president's speeches played a role in affecting support. At this point in time, the terror thematic frame came into greater public salience.

TERROR FRAME

Throughout 2003 and 2004, the terror theme continued as support for the war began to trickle away. Following the prospect theory argument that people inflate potential losses, it was important to frame and associate the Iraq war with the global war on terrorism, which was yet to be won. By maintaining the focus on what the public readily perceived as an enemy that could still strike without warning, as it did on September 11, the costs of the ongoing Iraq war could be perceived as worthwhile if the United States was avoiding future losses in the global war on terror. This approach followed the effective use of framing in rallying support for the Iraq invasion and continued through the U.S.-led occupation and rebuilding of Iraq. The following examples of terror framing occurred in numerous speeches in October, immediately after the U.S. casualty milestone. They show how the president reinforced and linked America's global war on terror with the war in Iraq:

> The war on **terror** has set urgent priorities for America abroad. We are not waiting while dangers gather. Along with fine allies, we are waging a global campaign against **terrorist** networks—disrupting their operations, cutting off their funding, and we are hunting down their leaders one-by-one. We are enforcing a clear doctrine: If you harbor a **terrorist**, if you feed a **terrorist**, if you support a **terrorist**, you're just as guilty

as the **terrorists**, and you can expect to share their fate. We're determined to prevent **terror** networks from gaining weapons of mass destruction. We're committed to spreading democracy and tolerance. As we hunt down the **terrorists**, we're committed to spending—spreading freedom in all parts of the world, including the Middle East. By removing the tyrants in Iraq and Afghanistan who supported **terror** and by ending the hopelessness that feeds **terror**, we're helping the people of that regime, and we're strengthening the security of America.[6]

In Afghanistan and Iraq, we gave ultimatums to **terror** regimes. Those regimes chose defiance, and those regimes are no more. (Applause.)[7]

We are aggressively striking the **terrorists** in Iraq. We will defeat them there so that we do not have to face them in our own country. (Applause.) We continue to call on other nations to help build a free country in Iraq. After all, it will make the world more secure when this happens.[8]

We are confronting that danger in Iraq where Saddam Hussein holdouts and foreign **terrorists** are desperately trying to throw Iraq into chaos by attacking coalition forces and international aid workers and innocent Iraqis. They know that the advance of freedom in Iraq would be a major defeat in the cause of **terror**. This collection of killers is trying to shake the will of America and the civilized world, and this country will not be intimidated. (Applause.) We are aggressively striking the **terrorists** in Iraq, defeating them there so we will not have to face them in our own country.[9]

And we have fought the war on **terror** in Iraq. The regime of Saddam Hussein possessed and used weapons of mass destruction, sponsored **terrorist** groups, and inflicted **terror** on its own people. Nearly every nation recognized and denounced this threat for over a decade. Last year, the U.N. Security Council—in Resolution 1441—demanded that Saddam Hussein disarm, prove his disarmament to the world or face serious consequences. The choice was up to the dictator, and he chose poorly.[10]

As the pre-invasion data showed, the U.S. war on terror issue was effective in promoting the theme to the American people. It represented one of the three frames in the triangle of effective thematic framing during the build-up to war: terror, WMDs, and threat. The effectiveness of Bush's October message was confirmed by a recovery in the polls. The president's message that the war in Iraq played a key role in the broader U.S. war on terrorism resonated well with the American public. The data shows that while the U.S. casualty milestone temporarily hurt support for the president and the Iraq war, the ratings recovery follows the terror framing frequency increase.[11]

Support for the war in Iraq and support for the president were vulnerable to significant impact from exogenous events such as casualty rates, although sometimes only temporarily; support for the global war on terror remained fairly steady and dropped below majority levels only once, in June 2004. For the American public, the war on terror had greater staying power. Consequently, the continued salience and public support for the war on terror issue became the key theme in gaining majority support for the war in Iraq and for Bush as those ratings began to fall to relatively critical levels in an election year.

LOSS DOMAIN

Loss domain terms continued to decline postinvasion and hit a low in August 2003 (Figure 6.1).[12]

After the September milestone and the U.S. combat deaths increase, the loss domain rhetoric, along with other thematic frames, continued to increase steadily and peaked prior to presidential elections. During the presidential elections, public support for keeping troops in Iraq increased to just above majority levels, while support for bringing troops home decreased to just below majority levels.[13] The slight advantage gained provided just enough support on the margins to continue the policy.

It is interesting that the rhetoric increases did not begin until the September U.S. casualty milestone, after which the remarketing of the war on terror now playing out in Iraq steadily increased until the big push prior to the 2004 elections. Therefore, while trying to garner greater support for the war, the president did not choose to highlight discussion of winning the war as much as relating Iraq to the larger threat of terrorism. The marketing effort in October 2004 precedes the public opinion rise, which was enough for the president to gain majority support.

According to most of the public opinion data cited, for loss and thematic framing to be effective, the effort has to occur on a large scale, as was seen in October–November 2002, September 2003, and prior to the 2004 elections. Slight increases in rhetoric do not influence public opinion changes; however, widespread and intense campaigns do, as was the case prior to the 2004 elections.

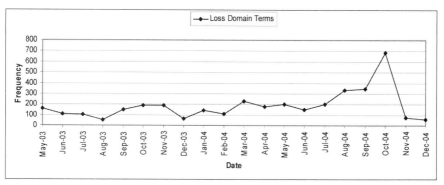

Figure 6.1   Loss Domain Terms

GAIN FRAMES

Following the cost-benefit logic, illustrated in Gelpi and Feaver's argument that "if and when the public is optimistic about a successful outcome, it is far more willing to bear the human cost of war," it would be expected to find more focus on U.S. victories and winning Iraq war.[14] While Bush's speeches have an increased amount of references to this theme, content analysis results showed that in comparison to discussion of the continuing war on terror, there was relatively little significant mention of victory and success, which is in accordance with prospect theory. The president kept the war on terror and the threat of terrorism salient as a potential future loss (Table 6.1).

While the terror frame frequency increased from 142 to 434 by October, the victory and win frames increased from 5 and 6 to 29 and 26, respectively.[15] If Gelpi and Feaver's proposition is correct, that Americans are defeat-phobic and discussion of gains will increase their support for war, then it would be expected that while public support for the Iraq war and the president was beginning to slip, we should see a dramatic increase in attempts to counterframe perceptions of what was beginning to be perceived as a declining issue for the president.[16] Significant increases in victory framing did not occur until just prior to Bush's election, yet their frequency continued to pale in comparison to loss rhetoric and the terror theme. Since we know that people focus on loss frames more than gain frames, then it would be expected that themes about victory in Iraq and Afghanistan would need to outnumber loss and terror themes. The data show the opposite occurred (Table 6.1).

While Gelpi and Feaver argued that the American public needs to perceive success or progress in order to continue to pay costs, the data showed that Bush's speeches continued to focus mostly on discussing losses and the ongoing terrorist issue, linking the speeches with a moderate ratings recovery. As an observable

Table 6.1   Gain and Loss Evaluation Frames Data Comparison

Date	Loss Domain Terms	Terror	Threat	Victory	Win
Jul-02	106	113	55	5	29
Aug-02	135	118	29	4	33
Sep-02	186	178	152	2	14
Oct-02	310	263	194	0	39
Nov-02	181	190	225	4	20
Dec-02	50	58	37	3	8
Jun-04	151	265	76	22	31
Jul-04	201	398	169	6	35
Aug-04	333	480	290	13	96
Sep-04	343	464	273	56	92
Oct-04	685	933	286	188	216
Nov-04	77	125	17	14	21
Dec-04	58	88	23	5	1

event, presidential cheerleading did not occur to a significant degree when compared to presidential nay-saying, nor does it show a strong association to changes
in public opinion polls.

PEACEFUL IRAQ AS CONTRADICTORY EVIDENCE

It is logical to expect a discussion of a peaceful Iraq to dominate Bush's rhetoric
if the cost-benefit argument were to provide contradictory evidence to prospect
theory. In the context of winning the war on terror in Iraq, Bush should have shown
a greater propensity toward discussing gains such as peace in Iraq as a result of the
U.S.-led invasion. A proximity search showed that at one point in August 2004,
discussion of peace in Iraq outranked discussion of terror in Iraq (Table 6.2).[17]

The peak in the peace in Iraq discussion comes much earlier than the peak in
the terror in Iraq discussion. The following excerpts highlight Bush's framing of
gains in Iraq:

> A free and peaceful Iraq and a free and peaceful Afghanistan will be powerful exam-
> ples in part of the world that is desperate for freedom.[18]

> See, a free and peaceful Iraq and a free and peaceful Afghanistan will be powerful
> examples to their neighbors. Free countries do not export terror. Free countries listen
> to the dreams of their citizens. By serving the ideal of liberty, we're bringing hope to
> others, and that makes our country more secure. By serving the ideal of liberty, we're
> spreading peace. (Applause.)[19]

> We set a clear goal, and Iraq and Afghanistan will be peaceful and democratic coun-
> tries that are allies in the war on terror. We will meet that goal by helping secure their
> countries, to allowing a peaceful political process to develop, and by training Afghan
> and Iraqi forces so they can make the hard decisions, so they can defend their country
> against those who are preventing the spread of freedom.[20]

These excerpts show the beginnings of a change in rhetoric for Bush. He began
to highlight a clear goal and gains in Iraq. While this discussion of gains in Iraq

Table 6.2   Terror and Peace in Iraq Data Comparison

Date	terror Iraq	peace Iraq
Jun-04	15	13
Jul-04	10	21
Aug-04	20	**61**
Sep-04	15	22
Oct-04	**38**	20
Nov-04	5	1
Dec-04	2	2

did not dominate Bush's rhetoric, it does represent the potential for contradictory evidence to the prospect theory approach to framing, as presented in this study.

At the same time, it is necessary to note that at some point in 2004, Peter Feaver, the key scholar positing a more gains-oriented approach to presidential framing of war, became employed by the Bush administration. His key role within the administration focuses on changing presidential war rhetoric to concentrate more on future gains rather than losses.[21] This issue is indicative of the many complex problems faced in social science research. While Bush's rhetoric showed the beginning of changes as a result of one scholar's influence, this study holds speech writers as constant and thus cannot exclude the change toward an increase in gain frames. However, the change toward gain frames was not dominant immediately prior to election month, when critical changes in public support occurred.

ELECTION CAMPAIGN

While support for the war in Iraq fluctuated and slowly declined with changes in rhetoric and exogenous events such as U.S. casualty milestones in September and the capture of Saddam Hussein in December 2003, a steadfast majority of Americans supported the U.S. war on terror. It is no wonder then that the president's public communication on the Iraq rebuilding efforts focused on linking the war in Iraq with the more global war on terror even more strongly than during the build-up to war during fall 2002 (Table 6.3).

Table 6.3   Gain and Loss Evaluations

Date	Terror	Threat	Victor	Win
Aug-03	142	26	5	6
Sep-03	251	36	18	19
Oct-03	**434**	73	**29**	**26**
Nov-03	273	50	15	**30**
Dec-03	72	28	12	11
Jan-04	139	43	16	32
Feb-04	137	67	6	21
Mar-04	272	147	23	53
Apr-04	273	157	10	40
May-04	248	100	20	67
Jun-04	265	76	22	31
Jul-04	**398**	**169**	6	35
Aug-04	**480**	**290**	13	**96**
Sep-04	**464**	**273**	**56**	**92**
Oct-04	**933**	**286**	**188**	**216**
Nov-04	125	17	14	21
Dec-04	88	23	5	1

Beginning in the summer of 2004, Bush put forth a similar but more encompassing strategy in earning majority support for the Iraq war through the global war on terror. Focus on threat framing decreased, relatively, but focus on the global war on terrorism increased to record levels. In October 2001, Bush mentioned terrorism 283 times, a peak for 2001. In October 2002, leading up to the Iraq war, he mentioned terrorism 263 times, a record for that year. In October 2003, immediately after the 1000-casualty milestone, he mentioned terrorism 434 times. However, in October 2004, just prior to the elections, mention of terrorism hit an all-time high of 933 times. This was indicative of Bush's latest and most concentrated war marketing campaign. As the data will show, discussion of having won the war on terror was negligible. At the same time, we see that according to some polls, as the rhetoric increased so did the approval ratings, regardless of mounting casualties. According to a *Washington Post*-ABC News poll, the percentage of Americans polled that approved of the war on terror increased by 10 percent to a total of 60 percent from June to August 2004. Despite a postelection decline in December, support levels remained above 50 percent.[22] Furthermore, the TIPP Presidential Leadership Index recorded a significant increase in President Bush's leadership performance. Bush's ratings rose from 47 percent in June to 53 percent, just above majority level, in November.[23] The public opinion data show significant causality from presidential speech content. This result had lasting effect on support for the U.S.-led war on terror well into President Bush's second term in office.

SUMMER 2004

By August 2004, support for the decision to go to war with Iraq dipped to 49 percent.[24] At the same time, a majority of Americans continued to believe that prior to the U.S. invasion, Iraq possessed WMD; 43 percent continued to perceive the administration as stating that Iraq gave direct support to al-Qaeda and 27 percent perceived that Iraq had direct involvement in the September 11 attacks.[25] These surprising public opinion results show that effective thematic framing carries a long shelf life within the public consciousness. However, for the first time, 52 percent stated that it would have been better to focus resources on pursuing al-Qaeda and stabilizing Afghanistan than to going to war in Iraq.[26] At the same time, a majority of Americans believed that the United States was winning the war on terrorism and that al-Qaeda was weaker now then before September 11. Additionally, according to the Pew Research Center, more Americans believed that the U.S. invasion of Iraq helped, rather than hurt, the war on terror.[27]

With public support for the war in Iraq dropping below majority levels and terrorism remaining salient in the public purview, the president had few viable options but to focus on reasserting the terrorism theme in order to gain support for his Iraq policy and his handling of the presidency. From August to October 2004, Bush began his largest marketing campaign. The thematic frame was simple, repetitive and widely disseminated on the campaign trail—the United States was now fighting the war on terror in Iraq as well as Afghanistan.

> When it comes to fighting the **threats** of our world, when it comes to making America safer, when it comes to spreading peace, we're moving forward, and we're not turning back. (Applause.) We've got more to do. I'm running for four more years because we've got more to do. (Applause.) We must continue to work with our friends and allies around the world to aggressively pursue the **terrorists** in Iraq and Afghanistan and elsewhere.[28]

> Yet, he had the capability to make weapons of mass destruction, and he could have easily shared that capability with **terrorist** enemies. Knowing what I know today, I would have taken the same action. America and the world are safer because Saddam sits in a prison cell. (Applause.) . . . Listen, I'm running for four more years because there's more work to do. We'll work with our friends and allies around the world to aggressively pursue the **terrorists** in Iraq and Afghanistan and elsewhere.[29]

> See, you can't talk sense to these people. You can't negotiate with these people. You cannot hope that they change. We will aggressively pursue them. We will engage them. **We will defeat them so we do not have to face them here at home**. (Applause.)[30]

> So I had a choice to make. Do I trust a madman and forget the lessons of September the 11th, or take action necessary to defend America? Given that choice, I will defend our country every time. (Applause.) Even though we did not find the stockpiles that we expected to find, Saddam Hussein had the capability of making weapons of mass destruction and could have passed that capability on to our enemy, and that was a risk we could not afford to take. Knowing what I know today, I would have made the same decision. (Applause.) . . . I'm running because I understand we must continue to work with our allies and friends to aggressively pursue the **terrorist** enemy in Iraq and Afghanistan and elsewhere. See, you can't talk sense to these people. You cannot negotiate with them. You cannot hope for the best. **We must aggressively pursue them around the world so we do not have to face them here at home**. (Applause.)[31]

> Our strategy is succeeding. Four years ago, Afghanistan was the home base of al Qaeda, Pakistan was a transit point for **terrorist** groups, Saudi Arabia was fertile ground for **terrorist** fundraising, Libya was secretly pursuing nuclear weapons, Iraq was a gathering **threat** and al Qaeda was largely unchallenged as it planned attacks. Because we acted, the government of a free Afghanistan is fighting **terror**, Pakistan is capturing **terrorist** leaders, Saudi is making raids and arrests, Libya is dismantling its weapons programs, The army of a free Iraq is fighting **terror** and more than three-quarters of al Qaeda's key members have been brought to justice. (Applause.)[32]

> We've led. Many have joined. And America and the world are safer. We've still got hard work. This progress involved careful diplomacy, clear moral purpose and some hard decisions—the hardest came on Iraq. We knew Saddam Hussein's record of aggression. We knew he was a sworn enemy of America. We knew of his support

for **terror**. After all, he harbored Abu Nidal, the leader of a **terrorist** organization that carried out attacks throughout Europe and Asia. Abu Abbas was in his country. He's the person that killed Leon Klinghoffer. Zarqawi, the beheader, had been in Baghdad prior to our arrival. We knew Saddam Hussein's long history of pursuing and even using weapons of mass destruction. We knew that. And we know that after September the 11th, our country must think differently. We must take **threats** seriously before they—before they fully materialize. (Applause.)[33]

In this dangerous world, we must never forget the lessons of September the 11th. We have a duty to protect the American people. We must take each **threat** seriously. So in Saddam Hussein we saw a **threat**, and I went to the Congress. The Congress looked at the intelligence I looked at, remembered the same history I remembered, and voted overwhelmingly to authorize the use of force. My opponent looked at the same intelligence I looked at, and he voted "yes" when it came time to authorize the use of force.[34]

If we stop fighting the **terrorists** in Iraq, they would be free to plot and plan attacks elsewhere, in America and other free nations. To retreat now would betray our mission, our word and our friends.[35]

The army of a free Iraq is fighting **terror**; and three quarters of al Qaeda's leadership have been brought to justice. (Applause.) This progress involved careful diplomacy, clear moral purpose, and some tough decisions—the toughest came on Iraq. We knew Saddam Hussein's record of aggression and support for **terror**. We knew that. I want you to remember that he harbored Abu Nidal, the leader of a **terrorist** organization that carried out attacks in Europe and Asia. We knew he harbored Abu Abbas, who killed American Leon Klinghoffer because of his religion. Zarqawi was in and out of Baghdad. He ordered the killing of an American citizen from Baghdad. We knew Saddam Hussein's long history of pursuing and using weapons of mass destruction. We knew that he would hope the world would turn away and not pay attention to him. We also knew that we must think differently after September the 11th. This country must take **threats** seriously before they fully materialize. (Applause.) That is a lesson we must never forget.[36]

I understand some Americans have strong concerns about our role in Iraq. I respect the fact that they take this issue seriously. It's a serious matter. I assure them we're in Iraq because I deeply believe it is necessary and right and critical to the outcome of the war on **terror**, and critical for long-term peace for our children and grandchildren. (Applause.)[37]

If another **terror** regime were allowed to emerge in Iraq, the **terrorists** would find a home and a source of funding and a source of support, and they would correctly conclude that free nations do not have the will to defend themselves. If Iraq becomes a free society at the heart of the Middle East, an ally in the war on **terror**, a model for hopeful reform in that region, the **terrorists** will suffer a crushing defeat. (Applause.) And that is why Democratic Senator Joe Lieberman calls Iraq "a crucial battle in the global war on **terrorism**." And that is why Prime Minister Tony Blair has called the struggle in Iraq "the crucible in which the future of global **terrorism** will be determined." That is why the **terrorists** are fighting with desperate cruelty—they know their future is at stake. Iraq is no diversion. It's a place where civilization is taking a decisive stand against chaos and **terror**, and we must not waver. (Applause.)[38]

Some excerpts contained loss and threat framing, but this was not as prevalent during the occupation and rebuilding phase as it was during the build-up to war. This made logical sense because while the president wanted people to inflate the potential loss of giving up on the war on terror, he did not want the public to be risk-acceptant enough to replace the incumbent president. As a result of the previously successful terrorism frame, there was no need to continue with ubiquitous loss framing to the same degree as before the invasion. Instead, the focus was on widening terrorism as a thematic frame, which played a crucial role in creating the focal lens for the actor to refocus the audience.[39]

In the postinvasion timeframe, the thematic framing consisted of focusing on policy attributes related to the U.S. war on terror, which was presented as inclusive of U.S. policy in Iraq. By organizing the Iraq-terrorism issue in this manner within the policy debate, the president focused on the importance of the war on terror as it pertained to Iraq. With support for the war on terror being higher than the war in Iraq, Bush was able to capitalize on terrorism's salience again, as he did in the fall of 2002, and gain adequate support for his foreign policy. Negative media coverage of the insurgency aimed at U.S. and coalition troops in Iraq helped further expand the terrorism issue and support the view that the United States was fighting a war on terror not only in Afghanistan but in Iraq as well.

The link to prospect theory exists because the terrorism theme had been previously introduced as a potential future loss, rather than a potential future gain. Thus, while the president discussed the ongoing war on terror as being far from over, the public continued to be placed below the aspiration level of winning the war on terror, thereby placing them in the domain of loss. By hyper-focusing on the terror theme, the president gained support for his policies and greater tolerance for the costs being expended. This occurrence runs counter to Gelpi and Feaver's argument that the public must see gains in order to be willing to expend the costs.

The majority of references to success, victory, and winning were unrelated to U.S. foreign policy and focused on the upcoming elections. The occurrence of win themes occurred in very small frequencies relative to the overall context of the ongoing war on terror. Typically, when they did occur in the context of foreign policy, the win and victory frames referred to winning the war on terror in the future as an aspiration level. While Bush did refer to future gains, future losses were even more present in the context of his speech. The following excerpt highlights winning the war on terror as a future aspiration and makes reference to future threats:

This new plan will help us fight and win the war on **terror**. This new plan will help us deal with the **threats** of the 21st century. It will strengthen our alliances while we build new partnerships to better preserve the peace. It will reduce the stress on our troops and on our military families. It was save the taxpayers money, as we consolidate and close bases and facilities overseas no longer needed to face the **threats** of our time and defend the peace and freedom of the world.[40]

The next excerpt is representative of statements made during Bush's reelection campaign and communicated frequently while on the campaign trail. Again, it refers to winning the war on terror at some point in the future: "We have more to do to wage and win the war against **terror**. America's future depends on our willingness to lead in this world. If America shows uncertainty and weakness in this decade, the world will drift toward tragedy. This is not going to happen on my watch."[41]

In general, winning the war on terror was the main theme throughout Bush's reelection campaign. The war in Iraq became part of that theme and Bush often discussed the war in Iraq and the war on terror as one:

> The biggest task we have in this country is to fight and win this war on **terror**. The most solemn duty a President has, the most solemn duty—(applause)—the most solemn duty those of us who hold high office have is to do everything we can to safeguard our country.[42]

> Someday—we will succeed in Iraq and Afghanistan by being firm in our beliefs, unyielding to the demands of those who want us to quit, those **terrorists** who are trying to kill people to get us to leave. That's what they're trying to do. We'll be successful. Everybody longs to be free. And when we are, we'll be able to look back and say, the world is better off. Someday, an American President and an Iraqi leader are going to sit down, talking about keeping the peace, talking about how to make a part of the world that is so desperate for freedom become a more peaceful place.[43]

As the terror theme increased to record levels, increases in future gain frames were also present:

> I think the next four years what you'll see is, because we're wiling to do hard work and stick to our word, and take action when necessary, and we've had a lot of successes, the next four years will be more peace. I think you're going to see the world changing for peace. And you've got to understand one reason why, and that's because there are just some fundamental values in life that are—that can change societies, starting with the thing that we take for granted in America, which is freedom.[44]

Gelpi and Feaver are correct, to a degree—discussion of winning and victory did become more frequent throughout Bush's speeches. However, if that were to have a greater effect than loss and terror framing then we would have seen a larger frequency of occurrence. In the end, it appears that people still hate to lose more than they like to win, which underscored much of Bush's war- and foreign policy–related campaign trail rhetoric.

EVE OF ELECTION

On the eve of the election, a significant number of Americans stated that if Saddam Hussein was not seeking WMDs and did not provide aid to al-Qaeda, then it was wrong to invade Iraq. However, a near majority still supported the decision to go to war.[45] Despite the Duelfer report, a majority of Americans still believed that Iraq was providing significant support to al-Qaeda and thus supported the war in Iraq.[46] The thematic frame linking the war on terror with Iraq was successful enough to withstand evidence to the contrary (mounting casualties and negative war coverage). At critical points in time, such as during the first Presidential Debate, the president highlighted that the war on terror was widespread, particularly in terms of geography:

> As a matter of fact, this is a global effort. We're facing a—a group of folks who have such hatred in their heart, they'll strike anywhere with any means. And that's why it's essential that we have strong alliances, and we do. That's why it's essential that we make sure that we keep weapons of mass destruction out of the hands of people like al Qaeda, which we are. But to say that there's only one focus on the war on terror doesn't really understand the nature of the war on **terror**.[47]

> The Philippines—we've got help—we're helping them there to bring—to bring al Qaeda affiliates to justice there. And, of course, Iraq is a central part of the war on **terror**. That's why Zarqawi and his people are trying to fight us. Their hope is that we grow weary and we leave. The biggest disaster that could happen is that we not succeed in Iraq. We will succeed. We've got a plan to do so. And the main reason we'll succeed is because the Iraqis want to be free.[48]

Here, the war on terror included various persons of interest:

> Of course, we're after Saddam Hussein—I mean, bin Laden. He's isolated. Seventy-five percent of his people have been brought to justice. The killer in—the mastermind of the September the 11th attacks, Khalid Shaykh Muhammad, is in prison. We're making progress. But the front on this war is more than just one place.[49]

In this excerpt, the president highlighted that winning was an aspiration level, required if the United States was to achieve security. While this showed a clearer plan to victory, it was done in the shadow of an elusive security:

> He believes, like I believe, that the Iraqis are ready to fight for their own freedom. They just need the help to be trained. There will be elections in January. We're spending reconstruction money. And our alliance is strong. That's the plan for victory. And when Iraq is free, America will be more secure.[50]

> And, of course, Iraq is a central part of the war on **terror**. That's why Zarqawi and his people are trying to fight us. Their hope is that we grow weary and we leave. The biggest disaster that could happen is that we not succeed in Iraq. We will succeed. We've got a plan to do so. And the main reason we'll succeed is because the Iraqis want to be free.[51]

My opponent calls Iraq a "great diversion" from the war on **terror**. I strongly disagree. The reason why Zarqawi is fighting so hard, why this **terrorist** is fighting so hard, is because he understands the stakes. A free Iraq will be a devastating blow for the ideologues of hate. He call it a diversion from the war on **terror**, I call it a battle in the war on **terror**. (Applause.)[52]

Again, while discussing success in the war on terror, the president put it in the context of not yet having achieved the ultimate goal, thereby leaving the United States vulnerable in the future. This was followed by the frequent statement of fighting terrorism abroad rather than fighting terrorism at home, in the loss frame context:

> We have had—we have had many victories in the war on **terror**. And that war goes on. Our nation is safer, but not yet safe. To win this war we must fight on every front. We will stay on the offensive against **terrorist** networks. We will strike them overseas so we do not have to face them here at home. (Applause.) We will confront governments that support **terrorists** and could arm them, because they're equally guilty of **terrorist** murder.[53]

Again, winning the war on terror was presented as an aspiration level rather than the status quo, insinuating that the status quo is in the domain of loss:

> America is always more secure when freedom is on the march. (Applause.) And freedom is on the march—in Afghanistan, in Iraq, and elsewhere. There will be good days and there will be bad days in the war on **terror**. But every day we will show our resolve and do our duty to future generations of Americans. (Applause.) This nation is determined. We will stay in the fight until the fight is won. (Applause.)[54]

The record levels of framing did not lead to sweeping changes in public support. However, even in the face of increasing casualties, negative media coverage, and no clear sign of future victory, the majority of the polling data showed that leading right up to the election, support for the president and his foreign policies nudged toward and sometimes above majority levels.[55]

While a slight majority is not ideal for an incumbent president facing election month, it was enough to be reelected. The decreasing support for the war gave both candidates only two options for marketing their versions of future foreign policies: (1) cut losses and withdraw, or (2) reassert a new aspiration level and place the public in the domain of loss, willing to accept more risks and costs. In this sense, Bush was able to take the perception that the war in Iraq was not going well and manipulate the reference point. He first framed the war in Iraq as part of the war on terror. Then he established winning the war on terror as a future aspiration level. Overall, the majority support for the war on terror spilled over to the war in Iraq, creating just enough to gain majority support and win the election.

CONCLUSION

The polling data support the argument that thematic and evaluative framing of an issue contribute toward gaining presidential and foreign policy support. The initial framing of Iraq as a terrorist supporter withstood significant media coverage to the contrary. It is logical to argue that negative media coverage of the Iraq war, which focused on terrorist/insurgent attacks on U.S. troops, helped President Bush frame the rebuilding of Iraq as part of the war on terror.

A potential counterargument against the effectiveness of framing is that people simply rallied around the president's foreign policies because of the upcoming 2004 election. However, a Harris poll showed that there was no change in opinion immediately before and after the election and that people's attitudes on the war in Iraq remained the same regardless of the election or the fighting in Fallujah, which took place immediately after the election.[56] If the polling data are explanatory of the public in general, then it further supports the argument that Bush's framing played a role in maintaining support for the war in Iraq. It also shows that exogenous events, such as rallying behavior by the voters or increased fighting in Iraq, played less of a role than otherwise expected.

Another explanation may be that voters renewed their support for the president's policies because they saw the inherent value in expanding the war on terror into Iraq. However, that argument contains some inherent chronological issues with respect to the origins of key targets in the war on terror. At present, it is clear that Iraq is a hotbed of terrorist activity and some argue that it is providing a training ground for future terrorists.[57] Whether or not Iraq was a key state in the U.S. war on terror was at the center of the post–Iraq invasion controversy, thus making it unlikely that prior to Bush's rhetoric on the subject, the public perceived Iraq to be a sponsor of terrorism. Therefore, it is plausible to reason that without the president's framing of Iraq as a terrorist state, the public may not have been as likely to view Iraq as part of the relatively widely supported war on terror.

The cost-benefit calculation argument that the American public was defeat-phobic and needed to see a clear plan to victory also fails to be adequately represented in Bush's speeches. While there was an increase in the frequency of that theme, it failed to compete with the war on terror and future loss from terrorism themes that dominated Bush's rhetoric on the Iraq issue.

Overall, the causality between Bush's public statements and public opinion polls suggests that the president's framing of the Iraq-terrorism issue had significant effect in persuading the public to perceive the widely supported war on terror as inclusive of the war in Iraq. Regardless of whether framing effects were successful independent of other events, a slight majority of the public chose to reelect President Bush and support the continuation of that military engagement while still facing losses.

While this study does not encompass all of the issues that promote the support and continuation of war, it provides insight into the potential for a relationship between presidential framing and presidential level of support. Strong causal correlation between changes in war on terror framing and relative changes in the public's support for the president and his foreign policies present fertile ground for further examination of the effectiveness of framing.

Findings and Implications

THE OVERALL ANALYSIS of President Bush's nearly 1500 foreign and national security–oriented speeches led to six broad findings, which provide an improved explanation of the relationship between presidential framing and public support for war. First, as the debate over the president's evidence against Iraq may be fading, it appears as that first impressions matter when framing terrorism. It is advantageous for an actor to frame the policy debate early on and stay consistent, even in the face of contradictory evidence. The ambiguity of the war on terror frame also contributed to its long-term success.

President Bush's initial framing of the September 11 attacks was the launching point for the U.S. war on terror. The war on terror framing had a lasting impact on the audience and became the predominant organizing theme of the political debate. The inclusion of Iraq as part of the war on terror framing withstood significant public scrutiny and criticism prior to Bush's reelection. In that sense, it was possible for the president to achieve persistent brand recognition in organizing the public's perspective on the war on terror. The war on terror frame withstood public scrutiny and contradictory evidence and was successfully used to frame and continue two separate invasions. From the September 11 attacks until June 2005, public support for the war on terror never fell below 50 percent.[1]

The same did not hold true for Iraq war support. Majority public support held in the first year of the war, then it began to recede below majority levels shortly after Bush's reelection. In light of the continually decreasing Iraq war support, we can conclude that framing effects do not have an indefinite shelf life, especially if their themes fail to produce on promised results. Specifically, failure to find the WMDs smoking gun in Iraq led to a backlash from former war supporters, contributing to an erosion of the overall support for a war that was not progressing as well as anticipated. The significance of this finding is that framing effects can contribute to mobilizing short-term war support, but can also work to reduce long-term support if they are based on unfounded arguments.

The second finding contends that while exogenous events may be significant causal variables in gaining support for war, especially for punitive war against terrorists, how an actor frames those exogenous events is where framing has added explanatory value because it guides the public toward how they should view those events. It would be fallible to ignore the September 11 attacks as a salient event that increased public support for the president and for a punitive war. Polling data revealed that most Americans felt the severity of the crisis and were experiencing negative psychological effects as a result of the attacks, which placed them in the domain of loss and made them more risk-acceptant.[2] In that sense, although state leaders cannot control exogenous events, they can control how the public views those events in a manner that captures public sentiment and acts as a reminder of previously suffered losses. Consequently, first impressions matter when attempting to establish successful (salient and long-term) framing, which can withstand significant criticism. At the same time, it does not appear that framing is a result of endogeneity, or "a consequence, rather than a cause" of the dependent variable, which can be a problem in qualitative research.[3]

Third, an effective thematic frame can be used over the long term on issues that may not be directly linked to the original exogenous event. Bush's initial framing of the September 11 attacks as a terrorist act and the beginning of the U.S. war on terror allowed him to capitalize on his initial framing and expand the war on terror to Iraq, then justify an unexpected and costly occupation long after September 11 occurred.

In that sense, it can be argued that Bush's usage of the terror theme was an attempt to market new and unrelated foreign policies while taking advantage of the previous public support after the September 11 attacks. All of the empirical cases support the finding that President Bush frequently utilized various thematic frames. However, he used the terror frame more frequently as the timeline progressed (Figure 7.1).

Convincing the public to support a preemptive war provided more of a challenge than convincing them to support a punitive war after the September 11 attacks. Consequently, framing levels increased significantly during the build-up to war in Iraq, with the terror frame taking a significant lead. From September 11 to his reelection in fall 2004, the terror frame dominated Bush's public speeches. While the frequency of the term does not imply that it had a direct impact on public opinion, it does show that since Bush's initial framing of terrorism had a lasting impression with the public, the term was used to continue the theme first introduced immediately after September 11. As a thematic frame, Bush's war on terror still had some political capital and salience, even two years after its initial conception, to make the case for invading Iraq. Therefore, the frame that began as a relatively vague theme, without a coherent timeline or list of targets, helped carry Bush's rhetoric over the course of two separate invasions.

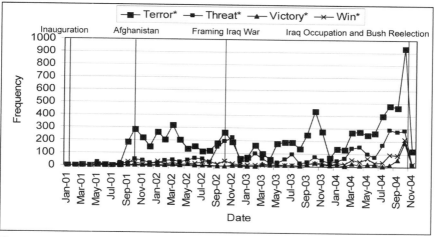

Figure 7.1   Bush Framing Chronology

While the extent of the war on terror evolved, it was the war's connection to the September 11 attacks that helped guide the American public in understanding future foreign policy changes. In the end, Americans' first impression of terrorism as the beginning of an uncertain war on terror mattered, even in light of evidence against expanding war aims.

The fourth finding suggests that a successful thematic frame can develop with a long-term loss evaluation. While the context surrounding the thematic frame can include an evaluation of a situation as a gain or a loss, themes developing over time can also cultivate an inherent but not necessarily permanent evaluation of the situation. For instance, when President Bush first introduced the U.S. war on terror, he referred to a punitive action for the losses suffered on September 11. During the build-up to war, the war on terror theme was used to encompass the possibility of war with Iraq. Post–Iraq invasion, the war on terror referred to the ongoing Iraq insurgency, which was magnified through media coverage of the unexpected resistance and mounting losses. In general, the president referred to the war on terror as something that required future costs, without setting a clear index or timeline for success.

As the war on terror grew, its meaning became associated with new targets and additional costs. At a certain point, the public became aware of themes that inherently referred to gains or losses. Through President Bush's rhetoric, the war on terror grew into an evaluation relative to the associated losses. While the president discussed the ongoing war on terror as being far from over, leading up to both Afghanistan and Iraq, the public continued to be placed below the aspiration level of winning the war on terror, thereby placing them in the domain of loss. Once the terror frame gained salience with the public, it also became a loss frame, bypassing the need to reestablish consistent loss evaluation framing. Since this finding refers to ongoing estimations by the public, it supports the argument that prospect theory applies to continuous decision making as well as single decisions.

Fifth, loss framing was more prevalent prior to policy execution while gain framing sometimes appeared after policy execution, thereby supporting the proposition that prospect theory tenets have better explanatory value than expected utility theory. While the original form of prospect theory was based on single decisions, over time, cumulative prospect theory stripped away the editing phase, the initial phase for decision making, and focused on the evaluation phase. Cumulative prospect theory is supported by public's long-term (albeit weak) support for the Iraq war, even when it was criticized for not going as well as planned.

Borrowing from behavioral finance literature, regret theory helps explain why even under present circumstances, the public shows only limited support for troop withdrawal. Based on the concept of cognitive dissonance, or the mental conflict experienced after a bad decision, regret theory argues that people fail to sell losing equity stocks as a result of regret over their bad decision.[4] In an effort to distance themselves from their bad decisions, people may stop being receptive to new contradictory information or create new arguments to maintain their previous beliefs.[5] Accepting losses in order to reduce cognitive dissonance is considered less than rational behavior.

Given that this behavior exists in the stock market, it is plausible to argue that the public similarly makes less than fully rational expected utility calculations in the political arena. Depending on the specific measure of progress, a majority of Americans believe that the United States is making progress and will succeed in Iraq. Moreover, a majority of Americans oppose withdrawing troops from Iraq. Of those that support a troop withdrawal, only a small minority (17 percent) supports an immediate withdrawal as opposed to one within the next one to two years.[6] At the same time, a majority of Americans believe that a U.S. troop withdrawal would further strengthen terrorism.

As President Bush's ratings hovered at 38 percent at the end of 2005, significantly lower than the slight majority at reelection time, the public continues to be optimistic about Iraq and sees potential losses if the United States were to withdraw from the country. The chronological description presented in this study supports the line of reasoning that Americans continue to hold on to the president's original thematic and evaluative framing of Iraq and America's war on terror, and are willing to continue to expend the necessary costs. At the same time, most Americans do not believe that President Bush has a clear plan for victory in Iraq.[7] This is consistent with this study's results of a greater loss to gain framing ratio, and consistent with the argument that gain framing is less relevant than loss framing with respect to public support for war.

As the public fears that a U.S. withdrawal from Iraq would lead to greater terrorism, Bush's loss frames continue to show considerable salience with the public, even as late as December 2005. While these results support the literature that public opinion is fairly stable, they do not support the findings that public opinion is rational. The public continues to support a costly war and focus on potential losses rather than gains.

The sixth and last general finding touches on the issue of public determinacy in presidential foreign policy making. When it comes to foreign policy making, does the president follow public sentiment prior to making a decision, or does he attempt to rally support after the fact? Linkage between framing and public opinion showed a strong relationship at the margins and status quo–changing foreign policies were carried out and maintained. If the public was fully determinate in the process, then why didn't the United States invade Iraq prior to September 11, when it already had majority support for a multilateral invasion?[8] Is presidential rallying for changing the status quo a formality in the elite-dominated foreign policy realm? It is plausible to argue that even in a democracy, public opinion may not be a significant domestic source of foreign policy behavior; however, it may act as a limiting factor in foreign policy decisions.[9]

Some people support the president regardless of his decisions, which seems to be counterintuitive. Behavioral finance research shows that people stick to their decisions in order to reduce regret about less than ideal outcomes. Presidential framing may not cause great changes in public opinion, but it appears that it could make a difference on the margins, creating a tipping point of whether or not the president decides to pursue risky policy changes and whether or not he gets reelected. As the past several years have shown, in the foreign policy arena, the president has had a great deal of freedom to introduce status quo–changing policies while going on to win the reelection campaign with marginal support.

This study also contributes some limited findings regarding the public's perceived casualty phobia. A significant amount of research posits that the public behaves rationally, at least up to a point, and is thus able to assess troop casualties relative to acquired gains. Although the ongoing war in Iraq has had relatively limited troop casualties in comparison to World War II and U.S. military operations in Korea and Vietnam, it only showed a limited impact on public opinion in 2004 when U.S. casualty levels reached 1000. The slight drop in public support for the war and for the president recovered after a subsequent rise in presidential framing, even prior to the capture of Saddam Hussein at the end of that year. These limited results would suggest that during the earlier stages of wartime, public opinion is not highly sensitive to U.S. casualties. This tends to correspond with some of the literature arguing that the American public is not willing to sustain military casualties when the policy objective is to coerce regime change as opposed to restrain aggressive behavior of another state, except in cases where the target state is framed as a threat to the United States.[10]

At the same time, these findings are not intended to compete with Mueller's findings directly. While Mueller's research covers long-term wars with high casualty counts, this research makes claims regarding the buildup and early phases of war, not great power wars as a whole. Following that line of thinking, it is plausible that if U.S. involvement in Iraq was to continue indefinitely, resulting in tens of thousands of U.S. casualties, then Mueller's casualty aversion argument would have greater explanatory value of the Iraq war as a whole, without discounting this research focus on earlier stages of build-up and policy execution. This study's findings can be used in evaluating past short-term military engagements, much like those implemented during the Clinton administration.

POLICY IMPLICATIONS

If the findings regarding the public's acceptance of low-level casualties—relative to cases such as U.S. involvement in World War II, Korea, and Vietnam—are robust, then the evidence also runs counter to the type of casualty aversion observations recorded during America's humanitarian operations in the post–Cold War era, which may have significant policy implications for future low-level military operations abroad. For instance, the Clinton administration suffered in the polls after the now widely analyzed 1992–1993 U.S. action in Somalia. The infamous Mogadishu firefight took place from October 3, 1993, through October 4, and on October 7, President Clinton withdrew U.S. troops from Somalia. In that case, President Clinton did not frame U.S. operations in Somalia as a prevention of possible future threats by failed states against the United States. His policy was framed mainly as a humanitarian mission.[11] Consequently, President Clinton did not attempt to counterframe the situation, closing off any potential for a rebound in the polls as President Bush had experienced after the 1000-casualty marker in 2004.

The point made here is that properly framed policies, intended to avoid future losses instead of making gains only, may find more favor with an increasingly isolationist American public. If the American president has the political resources and initiative to weather through the almost inevitable instances of negative events, then the public's casualty aversion may be as short lived as it was just months prior to President Bush's reelection. This could have policy implications for the longevity and success of future short- to mid-term humanitarian and nation-building missions.

LIMITATIONS

Measuring and testing framing effects on public opinion presents numerous challénges. In general, public opinion data is disorganized and intended for the short-term purposes of journalists, not for long-term research.[12] Much of the data used here was selected because it contained long-term, multiyear polling in order to capture the broader framing trends with the logic that long-term framing was more likely to resonate with the public.

Much of the available polling data on the Bush presidency is focused on specific opinions of the president and his policies, while avoiding opinions of the president as a communicator of those policies. Therefore, this study did not capture the public's conscious opinion of his framing attempts. The most effective approach to capturing this relationship would have been to conduct a single public survey over the course of the presidency focusing on the public's reaction to presidential rhetoric.

With respect to speech selection, since this study was intended to capture presidential framing in a broad perspective, some of the included speeches may have been targeted to a limited audience, not the general public, thereby skewing the results. One way to control for speeches intended for a broader audience would be to base speech selection on the media's coverage of the speech, thereby also capturing the media effect.

The failure of the gain domain terms points to another significant issue in this study. While the president's usage of loss domain terms indicated a distinct pattern over time, gain domain terms fluctuated with little discernible pattern. It is possible that the gain domain terms are simply too ubiquitous in the English language to track presidential rhetoric. However, this result is supported in prospect theory literature, which shows that gain frames have less semantic weight with test subjects.[13] Since Kahneman and Tversky's research shows that the slope for loss is steeper than that for gains, it is expected that loss framing would resonate more widely than gain framing. Additionally, some scholars argue that within American political culture, the public tends to listen to criticism and negatively oriented rhetoric more closely than compliments.[14]

While framing may help the public organize and evaluate an issue, the evidence presented here lends support to the argument that public opinion plays a limited role in the elite dominated foreign policy process, at least in the early stages of war. Consequently, these results may aid in the isolation of more robust variables toward better assessing the relationship between presidential framing and public support for war, such as the role of actor credibility in successful framing and counterframing.

This study's sole focus on the president is another limitation of the findings. Realistically, one cannot ignore the president's advisors and their framing attempts. Also, while the assumption that the president's advisors will pursue similar foreign policy agendas can help mitigate this weakness to some degree, that assumption is weak as there are historical accounts of foreign policy disagreements among advisors. The main reason behind the exclusion of the rest of the administration is the already vast amount of data attributed to the president. Systematically including other foreign policy framers over the four-year period could triple the speech data set, without adding descriptive value to the findings, because behind-the-scenes disagreements within an administration rarely translate into public rhetoric.

The evidence presented in this study focuses on the president and ignores the media's framing of U.S. foreign policy options. Although some scholars do not view the media as having significant effect on public support for war, it is difficult to ignore the media and its ability to instantly communicate the micro-level effects of American foreign policy during this revival of globalized communications.

Within this debate, some scholars have posited that mass media's framing effects influence public opinion, which may in turn influence foreign policy outcomes. It may also be useful to turn the causal arrow and ask if public opinion in the United States, partly informed by media framing, restrains the president's ability to pursue effective foreign policies and to what extent, if any. One line of thinking may be that if the media provides a short-term and instantaneous view of an issue, then it may miss the long-term policy effect that political science scholars tend to focus on. Therefore, the public may miss foreign policies' ramifications by focusing on micro-level effects. If that becomes the case, as it may have been regarding U.S. involvement in Somalia, then public opinion of U.S. foreign policy can be hijacked by short-sighted media framing.

One potential for research along those lines would be to address the relationship between the media, public opinion, and presidential foreign policy decision making. The main focus would be on presidential foreign policy decision making as the key dependent variable, while the media and public opinion would be the intervening or explanatory variables. The methodological approach would combine content analysis of presidential speeches and media framing, and quantitative analysis of public opinion datasets. Case selection could be based on variance in public opinion and the media's framing of U.S. post–Cold War foreign policies. The intention would be to first assess whether or not public opinion restrains foreign policy in humanitarian, nation building, or security oriented foreign policy; and second to determine the media's role in each case.

FINAL CONCLUSION

The main purpose of this investigation was to explain how George W. Bush gained support for war in Afghanistan and Iraq through the use of framing. Presidential framing and rhetoric may have a significant and independent impact on support for risky and aggressive foreign policies, aside from the impact of exogenous events, such as progress toward success.

This study adds value in illustrating how analysis of the presidential framing process can be applied to real-world scenarios. While a direct causal relationship between framing and public support for war was not established, the evidence provided insight into the current president's successful framing attempts with respect to his war policies and made a case for a parallel causal relationship between framing and exogenous events. One of the operating assumptions of this study was that rhetoric plays a role in the president's ability to create consensus among the populace. This was especially appropriate in mobilizing support against a new but not clearly identifiable enemy.

Connections between framing and the public's receptiveness to those framing attempts showed trends and patterns in setting the public agenda and creating a type of brand for future foreign policies. President Bush's initial framing of the September 11 attacks promoted widespread brand recognition of the U.S. war on terror. Currently, there is no evidence that the president or any of his advisors were aware of framing effects or deliberately used loss framing to mobilize support for war. However, in 2005, President Bush reasserted an administration-wide policy of using the war on terror phrase in order to avoid a public perception of new changes in U.S. foreign policy.[15] This came shortly after Defense Secretary Donald H. Rumsfeld initiated the phrase "global struggle against violent extremism," which was short-lived. Therefore, it appears that the war on terror frame continues to be deliberately used to promote various U.S. foreign policies. Also, the war on terror frame is not likely to disappear anytime soon, as some political strategists have recognized the value and effectiveness of this organizing theme and plan on utilizing it in future policy debates.[16]

The speech analysis presented here can be useful in more systematically assessing the president's foreign policy signaling efforts. This approach allows the researcher to move beyond simply looking at how often the president discussed issues such as Iran or China and assert types of contextual evaluations applied to those issue areas. In that sense, this approach to framing analysis can provide insights into an administration's foreign policy options and how it chooses to signal those options.

Epilogue: Surge versus Withdrawal Debate

IN DECEMBER 2006, the political debate regarding the future of U.S. troop levels in Iraq began to enter mainstream media. The public debate focused on whether the United States should pursue troop increases in Iraq or plan for a gradual troop withdrawal. The president commented on the possibility of a surge only when questioned about it directly.[1] However, the publicly available Iraq Study Group Report, also released in December, concluded that the situation in Iraq was "grave and deteriorating" and suggested a troop deployment surge in order to deal with the increasing insurgency violence and to speed up the training of Iraqi troops. Together, these statements brought the future of America's foreign policy on Iraq to the forefront of public attention in 2007.[2] Presidential hopefuls Hillary Clinton, John McCain, and Barack Obama spurred the debate forward in the public realm, yet President Bush did not strongly push the issue with the American public. Publicly, the president made only minor references to the issue throughout the debate. From January to June 2007, he mentioned the troop surge only a handful of times, and those instances were mostly a response to journalists' questions rather than planned speeches. Therefore, President Bush did not make frequent framing attempts to gain public support for a U.S. troop increase in Iraq. However, in the few instances the issue was discussed, the president framed it in the context of future losses, not gains.

> As we have **surged** our forces, al Qaeda is responding with their own **surge**. Al Qaeda is ratcheting up its campaign of high-profile attacks, including deadly suicide bombings carried out by foreign terrorists. America responded, along with coalition forces, to help this young democracy, and a brutal enemy has responded, as well. These attacks are part of a calculated campaign to reignite sectarian violence in Baghdad, and to convince the people here in America that the effort can't succeed. We're also

seeing high levels of violence because our forces are entering areas where terrorists and militia once has sanctuary. As they continue to do so, our commanders have made clear that our troops will face more fighting and increased risks in the weeks and months ahead.[3]

But you're right, that's what the **surge** is intended to do, plus provide enough time for these Iraqi forces to step in, prevent the sectarian violence from spilling out of the capital. What's difficult is the fact that al Qaeda continues to kill. And it frustrates the Iraqi people, and it should frighten the American people that al Qaeda is active in Iraq looking for a safe haven from which to launch further attacks. And they're the primary— they're the ones primarily responsible for these EID and suicide bombers.[4]

References to "reigniting sectarian violence" and the likelihood of "more fighting and increased risks in the weeks and months ahead" placed the surge issue in the context of future losses. While President Bush also added gain frames when discussing progress in Iraq, he poignantly stated that al-Qaeda is responsible for attacks against U.S. troops, and the terrorists' ability to freely operate should frighten the American people. These framing examples followed previous presidential attempts at increasing public support for foreign policy changes, but the relative infrequency of the attempts proved ineffective in raising public support for the troop surge.

Most of the presidential candidates took advantage of the issue and framed their positions toward a troop withdrawal. Barack Obama favored a withdrawal,[5] reflecting a growing sentiment among Americans.[6] Hillary Clinton also supported a troop withdrawal, although she continued to be hounded by her earlier support for the 2002 Iraq Resolution, which paved the way for President Bush to move forward with his Iraq policy.[7] John McCain was the only leading candidate to publicly support a troop surge, but only 36 percent of those polled believed that a surge would be effective.[8] None of the candidates expected a troop withdrawal to occur in the near future, but their framing of the issue reflected a growing majority consensus among the American public.

At the same time and while support for the war was decreasing, a near majority of 40 percent of Americans believed that the situation in Iraq was going very or fairly well.[9] This public opinion data is indicative of the parallel and sometimes contradictory opinions among Americans throughout the war. Accordingly, it would be fair to conclude that although support for the president's surge policy faltered amidst limited framing attempts, some presidential framing effect leftover was still evident as recently as March 2007, with a near majority perceiving the war effort in Iraq to be progressing forward.[10] Furthermore, it would also be fair to reiterate the point that foreign policy and tactical-level changes do not always depend on domestic public opinion. At the time of this writing, both the troop withdrawal debate and the troop surge occurred concurrently.

Notes

Chapter 1

1. Colin Dueck, "Ideas and Alternatives in American Grand Strategy, 2000–2004," *Review of International Studies* 30 (2004): 527.

2. Stephen M. Walt, "Beyond Bin Laden: Reshaping U.S. Foreign Policy," *International Security* 26, no. 3 (2001): 64.

3. Ole Weaver, "European Integration and Security: Analysing French and German Discourses on State, Nation, and Europe," in *Discourse Theory in European Politics*, ed. David R. Howarth and Jacob Torfing (New York: Palgrave Macmillan, 2005).

4. Mirjana N. Dedaic and Daniel N. Nelson, *At War with Words* (Berlin; New York: Mouton de Gruyter, 2003), xiii.

Chapter 2

1. William A. Boettcher and Michael D. Cobb, "Echoes of Vietnam?: Casualty Framing and Public Perceptions of Success and Failure in Iraq," *Journal of Conflict Resolution* 50 (2006), William A. Boettcher III, "Military Intervention Decisions Regarding Humanitarian Crises: Framing Induced Risk Behavior," *Journal of Conflict Resolution* 48, no. 3 (2004), Daniel Kahneman and Amos Tversky, "Choices, Values and Frames," *American Psychologist* 39 (1984), Daniel Kahneman and Amos Tversky, "Prospect Theory: An Analysis of Decision under Risk," *Econometrica: Journal of the Econometric Society* 47, no. 2 (1979), Rose McDermott, "Prospect Theory in Political Science: Gains and Losses from the First Decade," *Political Psychology* 25, no. 2 (2004), Richard H. Thaler et al., "The Effect of Myopia and Loss Aversion on Risk Taking: An Experimental Test," *Quarterly Journal of Economics* 112, no. 2 (1997), A. Tversky and D. Kahneman, "Advances in Prospect Theory—Cumulative Representation of Uncertainty," *Journal of Risk and Uncertainty* 5, no. 4 (1992).

2. Kahneman and Tversky, "Prospect Theory: An Analysis of Decision under Risk," George A. Quattrone and Amos Tversky, "Contrasting Rational and Psychological Analyses of Political Choice," *American Political Science Review* 82, no. 3 (1988).

3. Robert Jervis, "Political Implications of Loss Aversion," *Political Psychology* 13, no. 2 (1992), Miles Kahler, "Rationality in International Relations," *International Organization* 52, no. 4, International Organization at Fifty: Exploration and Contestation in the Study of World Politics (1998): 925–929, James G. March and Simon A. Herbert, *Organizations*, 2nd ed. (Cambridge, MA: Blackwell Publishers, 1993), 159–160, Jonathan Mercer, "Rationality and Psychology in International Politics," *International Organization* 59 (Winter 2005).

4. Kahneman and Tversky, "Prospect Theory: An Analysis of Decision under Risk."

5. Jervis, "Political Implications of Loss Aversion."

6. M. Friedman, *A Theory of the Consumption Function* (Princeton, NJ: Princeton University Press, 1957).

7. Donald P. Green and Ian Shapiro, *Pathologies of Rational Choice: A Critique of Applications in Political Science* (New Haven, CT.: Yale University Press, 1994), 289.

8. Alex Mintz, "Foreign Policy Decisionmaking: Bridging the Gap between the Cognitive Psychology and Rational Actor 'Schools'," in *Decisionmaking on War and Peace: The Cognitive-Rational Debate*, ed. Nehemia Geva and Alex Mintz (Boulder, CO: Lynne Rienner Publishers, 1997).

9. Graham T Allison and Phillip Zelikow, *Essence of Decision: Explaining the Cuban Missile Crisis*, 2nd ed. (New York: Addison Wesley Longman, 1999), Graham T. Allison, "Conceptual Models and the Cuban Missile Crisis," *American Political Science Review* 63, no. 3 (1969).

10. James G. March, *A Primer on Decision Making: How Decisions Happen* (New York: Free Press, 1994), 3.

11. Green and Shapiro, *Pathologies of Rational Choice: A Critique of Applications in Political Science*, 15, James D. Morrow, "A Rational Choice Approach to International Conflict," in *Decision Making on War and Peace: The Cognitive-Rational Debate*, ed. Nehemia Geva and Alex Mintz (Boulder, CO: Lynne Rienner Publishers, 1997), 14.

12. Mintz, "Foreign Policy Decisionmaking: Bridging the Gap between the Cognitive Psychology and Rational Actor 'Schools'," 5.

13. James D. Morrow, "Bargaining in Repeated Crises: A Limited Information Model," in *Models of Strategic Choice in Politics*, ed. Peter C. Ordeshook (Ann Arbor: University of Michigan Press, 1989), Herbert Simon, "A Behavioral Model of Rational Choice," *Quarterly Journal of Economics* 69 (1955): 10, Herbert Simon, "Human Nature in Politics: The Dialogue of Psychology with Political Science," *American Political Science Review* 79 (1985).

14. Cited in Rose McDermott, *Risk-Taking in International Politics: Prospect Theory in American Foreign Policy* (Ann Arbor: University of Michigan Press, 1998).

15. For a more detailed overview of prospect theory's tenets see Kahneman and Tversky, "Prospect Theory: An Analysis of Decision under Risk."

16. Bruce Bueno de Mesquita, *Principles of International Politics: People's Power, Preferences and Perceptions* (Washington, DC: CQ Press, 2000), 27, Benjamin A. Most and Harvey Starr, *Inquiry, Logic and International Politics* (Columbia: University of South Carolina, 1989), 27.

17. For decision-making analysis using formal theory see Claudio Cioffi-Revilla, *Politics and Uncertainty: Theory and Applications* (New York: Cambridge University

Press, 1998), Michael Nicholson, *Formal Theories of International Relations* (New York: Cambridge University Press, 1989).

18. Allison and Zelikow, *Essence of Decision: Explaining the Cuban Missile Crisis*, 52–53, Kahler, "Rationality in International Relations," 926–927, Herbert Simon, "Rationality in Political Behavior," *Political Psychology* 16 (1995): 46–47, Simon, "Human Nature in Politics: The Dialogue of Psychology with Political Science," 296.

19. Jack S. Levy, "An Introduction to Prospect Theory," *Political Psychology* 13, no. 2 (1992).

20. Kahneman and Tversky, "Choices, Values and Frames", Kahneman and Tversky, "Prospect Theory: An Analysis of Decision under Risk", Amos Tversky and Daniel Kahneman, "Rational Choice and the Framing of Decisions," *Journal of Business* 59, no. 4, part 2 (1986).

21. Kahneman and Tversky, "Choices, Values and Frames," 343, Tversky and Kahneman, "Rational Choice and the Framing of Decisions," S253.

22. Amos Tversky and Daniel Kahneman, "Loss Aversion in Riskless Choice: A Reference-Dependent Model," *Quarterly Journal of Economics* 106, no. 4 (1991).

23. Jack S. Levy, "Prospect Theory and International Relations—Theoretical Applications and Analytical Problems," *Political Psychology* 13, no. 2 (1992).

24. William A. Boettcher, "The Prospects for Prospect Theory: An Empirical Evaluation of International Relations Applications of Framing and Loss Aversion," *Political Psychology* 25, no. 3 (2004).

25. A. Tversky and D. Kahneman, "The Framing of Decisions and the Psychology of Choice," *Science* 211 (1981).

26. McDermott, *Risk-Taking in International Politics: Prospect Theory in American Foreign Policy*, 21.

27. Ibid., 22.

28. Boettcher, "The Prospects for Prospect Theory: An Empirical Evaluation of International Relations Applications of Framing and Loss Aversion."

29. See Maria Fanis, "Collective Action Meets Prospect Theory: An Application to Coalition Building in Chile, 1973–75," *Political Psychology* 25, no. 3 (2004), Barbara Farnham, "Roosevelt and the Munich Crisis—Insights from Prospect Theory," *Political Psychology* 13, no. 2 (1992), Rose McDermott, "Prospect-Theory in International-Relations—The Iranian Hostage Rescue Mission," *Political Psychology* 13, no. 2 (1992), McDermott, *Risk-Taking in International Politics: Prospect Theory in American Foreign Policy*, Kurt Weyland, "The Political Fate of Market Reform in Latin America, Africa, and Eastern Europe," *International Studies Quarterly* 42, no. 4 (1998).

30. David R. Mandel, "Gain-Loss Framing and Choice: Separating Outcome Formulations from Descriptor Formulations," *Organizational Behavior and Human Decision Processes* 85, no. 1 (2001).

31. X. T. Wang, "Self-Framing of Risky Choice," *Journal of Behavioral Decision Making* 17, no. 1 (2004).

32. Boettcher, "The Prospects for Prospect Theory: An Empirical Evaluation of International Relations Applications of Framing and Loss Aversion."

33. Jeffrey W. Taliaferro, "Quagmires in the Periphery: Foreign Wars and Escalating Commitment in International Conflict," *Security Studies* 7, no. 3 (1998).

34. Irwin P. Levin, Sandra L. Schneider, and Gary J. Gaeth, "All Frames Are Not Created Equal: A Typology and Critical Analysis of Framing Effects," *Organizational*

Behavior and Human Decision Processes 76, no. 2 (1998), Tversky and Kahneman, "The Framing of Decisions and the Psychology of Choice."

35. Levin, Schneider, and Gaeth, "All Frames Are Not Created Equal: A Typology and Critical Analysis of Framing Effects."

36. Nehemia Geva, Allison Astorino-Courtois, and Alex Mintz, "Marketing the Peace Process in the Middle East: The Effectiveness of Thematic and Evaluative Framing in Jordan and Israel," in *Arms Spending, Development and Security*, ed. Manas Chatterji, Jacques Fontanel, and Akira Hattori (New Delhi: APH Publishing, 1996), 362.

37. Ibid.

38. Jeffrey W. Taliaferro, "Power Politics and the Balance of Risk: Hypotheses on Great Power Intervention in the Periphery," *Political Psychology* 25, no. 2 (2004).

39. Ibid.

40. Daniel Kahneman and Amos Tversky, "Choices, Values, and Frames," in *Choices, Values, and Frames*, ed. Daniel Kahneman and Amos Tversky (Cambridge: Cambridge University Press, 2000), 2.

41. Paul Slovic, Baruch Fischhof, and Sarah Lichtenstein, "Facts versus Fears: Understanding Perceived Risk," in *Judgment under Uncertainty: Heuristics and Biases*, ed. Daniel Kahneman, Paul Slovic, and Amos Tversky (Cambridge: Cambridge University Press, 1982), 464.

42. Lydia Andrade and Garry Young, "Presidential Agenda Setting: Influences on the Emphasis of Foreign Policy," *Political Research Quarterly* 49, no. 3 (1996), Jeffrey E. Cohen, "Presidential Rhetoric and the Public Agenda," *American Journal of Political Science* 39, no. 1 (1995), Jeffrey S. Peake, "The Limits of Presidential Rhetoric: The Agenda-Setting Impact of Major Television Addresses" paper presented at the Annual Meeting of the American Political Science Association, 2003, John C. Tedesco, "Issue and Strategy Agenda-Setting in the 2000 Presidential Primaries," *American Behavioral Scientist* 44, no. 12 (2001).

43. Thomas J. Christensen, *Useful Adversaries: Grand Strategy, Domestic Mobilization, and Sino-American Conflict, 1947–1958* (Princeton, NJ: Princeton University Press, 1996).

44. For the most recent research into this issue, see Boettcher and Cobb, "Echoes of Vietnam?: Casualty Framing and Public Perceptions of Success and Failure in Iraq," Boettcher, "Military Intervention Decisions Regarding Humanitarian Crises: Framing Induced Risk Behavior."

45. Historical case study research involving prospect theory was first introduced in the work by McDermott, "Prospect-Theory in International-Relations—The Iranian Hostage Rescue Mission," McDermott, *Risk-Taking in International Politics: Prospect Theory in American Foreign Policy*.

46. A. M. Bayoumi and D. A. Redelmeier, "Decision Analysis with Cumulative Prospect Theory," *Medical Decision Making* 20, no. 4 (2000), H. Fennema and P. Wakker, "Original and Cumulative Prospect Theory: A Discussion of Empirical Differences," *Journal of Behavioral Decision Making* 10, no. 1 (1997), Lola L. Lopes and Gregg C. Oden, "The Role of Aspiration Level in Risky Choice: A Comparison of Cumulative Prospect Theory and Sp/a Theory," *Journal of Mathematical Psychology* 43, no. 2 (1999), W. Neilson and J. Stowe, "A Further Examination of Cumulative Prospect Theory Parameterizations," *Journal of Risk and Uncertainty* 24, no. 1 (2002), F. Philippe, "Cumulative Prospect Theory and Imprecise Risk," *Mathematical Social Sciences* 40, no. 3 (2000), U. Schmidt, "Reference Dependence in Cumulative Prospect Theory," *Journal of Mathematical*

Psychology 47, no. 2 (2003), P. P. Wakker and H. Zank, "A Simple Preference Foundation of Cumulative Prospect Theory with Power Utility," *European Economic Review* 46, no. 7 (2002), P. Wakker and A. Tversky, "An Axiomatization of Cumulative Prospect Theory," *Journal of Risk and Uncertainty* 7, no. 2 (1993).

47. William A. Boettcher III, "Context, Methods, Numbers, and Words: Prospect Theory in International Relations," *Journal of Conflict Resolution* 39, no. 3 (1995).

48. Gary Schaub, "Deterrence, Compellence, and Prospect Theory," *Political Psychology* 25, no. 3 (2004).

49. N. Barberis, M. Huang, and T. Santos, "Prospect Theory and Asset Prices," *Quarterly Journal of Economics* 116, no. 1 (2001), J. A. List, "Neoclassical Theory versus Prospect Theory: Evidence from the Marketplace," *Econometrica* 72, no. 2 (2004).

50. Geva, Astorino-Courtois, and Mintz, "Marketing the Peace Process in the Middle East: The Effectiveness of Thematic and Evaluative Framing in Jordan and Israel," A. Mintz and S. B. Redd, "Framing Effects in International Relations," *Synthese* 135, no. 2 (2003).

51. Paul Chilton, *Analysing Political Discourse Theory and Practice* (London: Routledge, 2004), 138.

52. Jennifer Milliken, "The Study of Discourse in International Relations: A Critique of Research and Methods," *European Journal of International Relations* 5, no. 2 (1999).

53. Ole R. Holsti, *Content Analysis for the Social Sciences and Humanities* (Reading, MA: Addison-Wesley, 1969).

54. Edward G. Carmines and Richard A. Zeller, eds., *Reliability and Validity Assessment*, vol. 17, *Quantitative Applications in the Social Sciences* (Sage Publications, 1979), 11–12.

55. Kahneman and Tversky, "Prospect Theory: An Analysis of Decision under Risk."

56. Barbara Ann Kipfer, ed., Roget's New Millennium™ Thesaurus, 1st ed. (Lexico Publishing Group, 2005).

57. Due to software restrictions, hyphenated terms cannot be used as search terms.

58. Mintz and Redd, "Framing Effects in International Relations," 195.

59. Farnham, "Roosevelt and the Munich Crisis—Insights from Prospect Theory," Jervis, "Political Implications of Loss Aversion," McDermott, "Prospect-Theory in International-Relations—the Iranian Hostage Rescue Mission," Tversky and Kahneman, "Rational Choice and the Framing of Decisions." Cited in Mintz and Redd, "Framing Effects in International Relations."

60. George W. Bush, Remarks by the President at U.S. Naval Academy Commencement (2001 [cited August 2005]); available online at www.whitehouse.gov/news/releases/2001/05/20010525-1.html.

61. George W. Bush, Remarks by the President at Memorial Day Commemoration (2001 [cited August 2005]); available online at www.whitehouse.gov/news/releases/2001/05/20010529-1.html.

62. George W. Bush, Remarks by the President at Camp Pendleton, California (2001 [cited August 2005]); available online at www.whitehouse.gov/news/releases/2001/05/20010529-6.html.

63. Bush, Remarks by the President at U.S. Naval Academy Commencement ([cited).

64. George W. Bush, President Stresses Volunteerism at Atlanta High School (2002 [cited August 2005]); available from http://www.whitehouse.gov/news/releases/2002/01/20020131-7.html.

65. Ibid.

66. George W. Bush, President Holds Town Hall Forum on Economy in California (2002 [cited August 2005]); available online at www.whitehouse.gov/news/releases/2002/01/20020105-3.html.

67. George W. Bush, President Urges Action on Economic Plan to Oregon Workers (2002 [cited August 2005]); available online at www.whitehouse.gov/news/releases/2002/01/20020105-6.html.

68. Ibid.

69. George W. Bush, President Meets with Economic Advisors and Federal Reserve Chairman Greenspan (2002 [cited August 2005]); available online at www.whitehouse.gov/news/releases/2002/01/20020107-3.html.

70. Mintz and Redd, "Framing Effects in International Relations," 195.

71. Kahneman and Tversky, "Prospect Theory: An Analysis of Decision under Risk."

72. Boettcher, "The Prospects for Prospect Theory: An Empirical Evaluation of International Relations Applications of Framing and Loss Aversion," 334.

73. For further discussion, see Grant N. Marshall, Lois M. Davis, and Cathy D. Sherbourne, A Review of the Scientific Literature as It Pertains to Gulf War Illnesses (2000 [cited 2006]); available online at www.rand.org/pubs/monograph_reports/MR1018.4-1. Actual U.S. troops began deploying to Kuwait in early January 2003. See Military News: Defense Policy/Programs (2003 [cited February 2006]); available online at www.globalsecurity.org/military/library/news/2003/01/01-03_index.htm#policy.

74. Adrian Edwards et al., "Presenting Risk Information—a Review of the Effects of "Framing" and Other Manipulations on Patient Outcomes.," Journal of Health Communication 6, no. 1 (2001), P Knapp, D K Raynor, and D C Berry, "Comparison of Two Methods of Presenting Risk Information to Patients About the Side Effects of Medicines," Qual Saf Health Care 13, no. 3 (2004).

Chapter 3

1. Carol Gelderman, *All the President's Words* (New York: Walker, 1997), 1.

2. Karlyn Kohrs Campbell and Kathleen Hall Jamieson, *Deeds Done in Words: Presidential Rhetoric and the Genres of Governance* (Chicago: University of Chicago Press, 1990).

3. While loss framing was used by other parties to either promote or restrain war, actors like Saddam Hussein prior to the 1991 Persian Gulf War and more recent antiwar groups did not have the same level of media access nor the built-in dominance that comes with presidential influence in the United States. See John Mueller, *Policy and Opinion in the Gulf War* (Chicago: University of Chicago Press, 1994), xiii, Paul E. Peterson, "The President's Dominance in Foreign Policy Making," *Political Science Quarterly* 109, no. 2 (1994).

4. Dan Reiter and Allan C. Stam, *Democracies at War* (Princeton, NJ: Princeton University Press, 2002).

5. Bruce Bueno de Mesquita et al., *The Logic of Political Survival* (Cambridge, MA: MIT Press, 2003), Kurt Taylor Gaubatz, *Elections and War: The Electoral Incentive in the Democratic Politics of War and Peace* (Stanford, CA: Stanford University Press, 1999).

6. Erik Voeten and Paul R. Brewer, "Public Opinion, the War in Iraq, and Presidential Accountability," *Journal of Conflict Resolution* 50, no. 6 (2006).

7. Ibid.

8. Bruce Russett and Thomas W. Graham, "Public Opinion and National Security Policy: Relationships and Impacts," in *Handbook of War Studies*, ed. Manus I. Midlarsky (Ann Arbor: University of Michigan Press, 1989), 239. While Russett and Graham refer to studies from the 1950s and 1960s as early public opinion studies, they call for a renewed interest into this research area as a result of greater access and availability of public opinion information.

9. Bruce Russett, *Controlling the Sword: The Democratic Governance of National Security* (Cambridge. MA: Harvard University Press, 1990), 91.

10. Ibid., 92, 95.

11. John Mueller, *War, Presidents, and Public Opinion* (New York: John Wiley and Sons, 1973), 65.

12. Ibid., 167.

13. John Mueller, "Public Support for Military Ventures Abroad," in *The Real Lessons of the Vietnam War: Reflections Twenty-Five Years after the Fall of Saigon*, ed. John Norton Moore and Robert F. Turner (Durham, NC: Carolina Academic Press, 2002), 183.

14. Eric V. Larson, *Casualties and Consensus: The Historical Role of Casualties in Domestic Support for U.S. Military Operations* (Santa Monica, CA: RAND, 1996), xv–xvi.

15. Christopher Gelpi, Peter Feaver, and Jason Reifler, "Success Matters: Casualty Sensitivity and the War in Iraq," *Journal of International Security* (Winter 2005/2006).

16. Peter Feaver and Christopher Gelpi, *Choosing Your Battles: American Civil-Military Relations and the Use of Force* (Princeton, NJ: Princeton University Press, 2004), 96–97.

17. Benjamin I. Page and Robert Y. Shapiro, *The Rational Public: Fifty Years of Trends in Americans' Policy Preferences* (Chicago: University of Chicago Press, 1992).

18. Bruce W. Jentleson, "The Pretty Prudent Public: Post Post-Vietnam American Opinion on the Use of Military Force," *International Studies Quarterly* 36 (1992).

19. Steven Kull and I. M. Destler, *Misreading the Public: The Myth of a New Isolationism* (Washington, DC: Brookings Institution Press, 1999).

20. Richard Sobel, *The Impact of Public Opinion on U.S. Foreign Policy since Vietnam* (New York: Oxford University Press, 2001).

21. Fareed Zakaria, "Realism and Domestic Politics: A Review Essay," review of *Myths of Empire: Domestic Politics and International Ambition*, by Jack Snyder, *International Security* 17, no. 1 (1992).

22. Kenneth N. Waltz, "Realist Thought and Neorealist Theory," in *Controversies in International Relations Theory: Realism and the Neoliberal Challenge*, ed. Charles W. Kegley (New York: St. Martin's Press, 1995).

23. Stephen Van Evera, "Offense, Defense, and the Causes of War," *International Security* 22, no. 4 (1998).

24. Robert Gilpin, *War and Change in World Politics* (Cambridge: Cambridge University Press, 1981).

25. Jack L. Snyder, *Myths of Empire: Domestic Politics and International Ambition, Cornell Studies in Security Affairs* (Ithaca, NY: Cornell University Press, 1991).

26. Will H. Moore and David J. Lanoue, "Domestic Politics and U.S. Foreign Policy: A Study of Cold War Conflict Behavior," *Journal of Politics* 65, no. 2 (2003).

27. Ethan Kapstein, "Is Realism Dead? The Domestic Sources of International Politics," *International Organization* 49 (1995).

28. Andrew Moravcsik, "Taking Preferences Seriously: A Liberal Theory of International Politics," *International Organization* 51, no. 4 (1997).

29. Helen V. Milner, *Interests, Institutions, and Information: Domestic Politics and International Relations* (Princeton, NJ: Princeton University Press, 1997).

30. Frank R. Baumgartner and Bryan D. Jones, "Representation and Agenda Setting," *Policy Studies Journal* 32, no. 1 (2004).

31. Frank R. Baumgartner and Bryan D. Jones, *Agendas and Instability in American Politics* (Chicago: University of Chicago Press, 1993), Cohen, "Presidential Rhetoric and the Public Agenda," Peterson, "The President's Dominance in Foreign Policy Making."

32. Jeffrey S. Peake, "Presidential Agenda Setting in Foreign Policy," *Political Research Quarterly* 54, no. 1 (2001).

33. Paul C. Light, *The President's Agenda: Domestic Policy Choice from Kennedy to Carter* (Baltimore, MD: Johns Hopkins University Press, 1982), James P. Pfiffner, *The Strategic Presidency: Hitting the Ground Running* (Chicago: Dorsey, 1988). Cited in Cohen, "Presidential Rhetoric and the Public Agenda."

34. John W. Kingdon, *Agendas, Alternatives, and Public Policies*, 2nd ed. (Boston: Little Brown, 1995), 148–149.

35. Peake, "Presidential Agenda Setting in Foreign Policy."

36. Cohen, "Presidential Rhetoric and the Public Agenda."

37. Roy L. Behr and Shanto Iyengar, "Television News, Real-World Cues, and Changes in the Public Agenda," *Public Opinion Quarterly* 49, no. 1 (1985).

38. Charles Cameron, John S. Lapinski, and Charles R. Riemann, "Testing Formal Theories of Political Rhetoric," *Journal of Politics* 62, no. 1 (2000).

39. Shanto Iyengar, "How Citizens Think about National Issues: A Matter of Responsibility," *American Journal of Political Science* 33, no. 4 (1989).

40. Edwards et al., "Presenting Risk Information—A Review of the Effects of 'Framing' and Other Manipulations on Patient Outcomes."

Chapter 4

1. Walt, "Beyond Bin Laden: Reshaping U.S. Foreign Policy."

2. *Economy, Education, Social Security Dominate Public's Policy Agenda,* Pew Research Center (2001 [cited August 2005]); available online at people-press.org/reports/display.php3?ReportID=4.

3. George W. Bush, Remarks by the President to Students and Faculty at National Defense University (2001 [cited August 2005]); available online at www.whitehouse.gov/news/releases/2001/05/20010501-10.html.

4. Stanley Feldman, ed., *Answering Survey Questions: The Measurement and Meaning of Public Opinion, Political Judgment: Structure and Process* (Ann Arbor: University of Michigan Press, 1995).

5. George W. Bush, Remarks by the President to Southwest Michigan First Coalition/Kalamazoo Chamber of Commerce Joint Event on the Economy (2001 [cited August 2005]); available online at www.whitehouse.gov/news/releases/2001/03/20010327-5.html, George W. Bush, Remarks by the President to the Greater Portland Chambers of Commerce Meeting (2001 [cited August 2005]); available online at www.whitehouse.gov/news/releases/2001/03/20010323.html.

6. Bush, Remarks by the President to Students and Faculty at National Defense University.

7. George W. Bush, Statement by the President: Domestic Preparedness against Weapons of Mass Destruction (2001 [cited August 2005]); available online at www.whitehouse.gov/news/releases/2001/05/20010508.html.

8. Bush, Remarks by the President to Students and Faculty at National Defense University.

9. Ibid.

10. Ibid.

11. Ibid.

12. Ibid.

13. George W. Bush, President George W. Bush's Inaugural Address (2001 [cited August 2005]); available online at www.whitehouse.gov/news/inaugural-address.html.

14. A National Security Strategy for a New Century (1998 [cited 2005]); available online at clinton2.nara.gov/WH/EOP/NSC/html/documents/nssr.pdf.

15. Peter Lavoy, "What's New in the New U.S. Strategy to Combat Wmd?," *Strategic Insights* I, no. 10 (2002).

16. Susan D. Moeller, *Media Coverage of Weapons of Mass Destruction* (Center for International and Security Studies at Maryland, 2004 [cited 2005]); available online at www.cissm.umd.edu/documents/WMDstudy_full.pdf.

17. Thomas H. Kean et al., "The Final Report of the National Commission on Terrorist Attacks upon the United States" (2004), 258–260.

18. George W. Bush, Remarks by the President to National Guard Personnel (2001 [cited August 2005]); available online at www.whitehouse.gov/news/releases/2001/02/20010214-2.html, George W. Bush, Remarks by the President to State Department Employees (2001 [cited August 2005]); available online at www.whitehouse.gov/news/releases/2001/02/20010215-5.html.

19. Bush, Remarks by the President to National Guard Personnel, Bush, Remarks by the President to State Department Employees.

20. Dueck, "Ideas and Alternatives in American Grand Strategy, 2000–2004," 524.

21. George W. Bush, Remarks by the President upon Arrival (2001 [cited July 2005]); available online at www.whitehouse.gov/news/releases/2001/09/20010916-2.html.

22. George W. Bush, President Launches Online American Relief and Response Effort (2001 [cited July 2005]); available online at www.whitehouse.gov/news/releases/2001/09/20010918-1.html.

23. George W. Bush, Remarks by the President at Photo Opportunity with House and Senate Leadership (2001 [cited July 2005]); available online at www.whitehouse.gov/news/releases/2001/09/20010919-8.html.

24. George W. Bush, At O'Hare, President Says "Get on Board" (2001 [cited July 2005]); available online at www.whitehouse.gov/news/releases/2001/09/20010927-1.html.

25. George W. Bush, President Bush Salutes Heroes in New York (2001 [cited July 2005]); available online at www.whitehouse.gov/news/releases/2001/09/20010914-9.html.

26. George W. Bush, President's Remarks at National Day of Prayer and Remembrance (2001 [cited July 2005]); available online at www.whitehouse.gov/news/releases/2001/09/20010914-2.html.

27. George W. Bush, President Urges Readiness and Patience (2001 [cited July 2005]); available online at www.whitehouse.gov/news/releases/2001/09/20010915-4.html.

28. George W. Bush, Address to a Joint Session of Congress and the American People (2001 [cited July 2005]); available online at www.whitehouse.gov/news/releases/2001/09/20010920-8.html.

29. Bush, President's Remarks at National Day of Prayer and Remembrance.

30. Ibid.

31. Bush, President Launches Online American Relief and Response Effort.

32. Bush, At O'Hare, President Says "Get on Board."

33. George W. Bush, Address to a Joint Session of Congress and the American People (2001 [cited August 2005]); available online at www.whitehouse.gov/news/releases/2001/09/20010920-8.html.

34. George W. Bush, President's Remarks at National Day of Prayer and Remembrance (2001 [cited August 2005]); available online at www.whitehouse.gov/news/releases/2001/09/20010914-2.html.

35. George W. Bush, Presidential Address to the Nation (2001 [cited August 2005]); available online at www.whitehouse.gov/news/releases/2001/10/20011007-8.html.

36. Bush, Address to a Joint Session of Congress and the American People.

37. Ibid.

38. George W. Bush, President: FBI Needs Tools to Track Down Terrorists (2001 [cited July 2005]); available online at www.whitehouse.gov/news/releases/2001/09/20010925-5.html.

39. George W. Bush, President Thanks CIA (2001 [cited July 2005]); available online at www.whitehouse.gov/news/releases/2001/09/20010926-3.html.

40. Economy, Education, Social Security Dominate Public's Policy Agenda.

41. Steven Kull, *Americans on the War on Terrorism: A Study of US Public Attitudes* (Program on International Policy Attitudes, 2001 [cited August 2005]); available online at www.pipa.org/OnlineReports/Terrorism/WarOnTerror_Nov01/WarOnTerror_Nov01_rpt.pdf, *Overwhelming Support for Bush, Military Response But . . . American Psyche Reeling from Terror Attacks,* Pew Research Center (2001 [cited August 2005]); available online at www.pewtrusts.com/ideas/ideas_item.cfm?content_item_id=749&content_type_id=18&issue_name=Public%20opinion%20and%20polls&issue=11&page=18&name=Public%20Opinion%20Polls%20and%20Survey%20Results#intro, *Washington Post*-ABC News Poll June 2005 (2005 [cited August 2005]); available online at www.washingtonpost.com/wp-dyn/content/article/2005/06/07/AR2005060700296.html, http://www.washingtonpost.com/wp-srv/politics/polls/postpoll050607.pdf.

42. Kull, *Americans on the War on Terrorism: A Study of US Public Attitudes.*

43. Ibid.

44. Ibid.

45. Bush, Address to a Joint Session of Congress and the American People.

46. *Overwhelming Support for Bush, Military Response But . . . American Psyche Reeling from Terror Attacks, Poll: Americans Taking Abramoff, Alito and Domestic Spying in Stride,* Pew Research Center (2006 [cited January 2006]); available online at www.pewtrusts.com/pdf/PRC_news_01106.pdf.

47. *Overwhelming Support for Bush, Military Response But . . . American Psyche Reeling from Terror Attacks.*

48. George W. Bush, President Holds Prime Time News Conference (2001 [cited August 2005]); available online at www.whitehouse.gov/news/releases/2001/10/20011011-7.html#.

49. George W. Bush, President Unveils "Most Wanted" Terrorists (2001 [cited August 2005]); available online at www.whitehouse.gov/news/releases/2001/10/20011010-3.html.

50. George W. Bush, President Reports Progress, Calls for Action in Cabinet Meeting (2001 [cited July 2005]); available online at www.whitehouse.gov/news/releases/2001/10/20011011-3.html.

51. Searches for terms with different word endings were executed as a wildcard searches *, for term variations such as terrorism, terrorist, etc.

52. Bush, Address to a Joint Session of Congress and the American People, Bush, Presidential Address to the Nation.

53. Bush, Address to a Joint Session of Congress and the American People.

54. George W. Bush, President: "We're Making Progress" (2001 [cited July 2005]); available online at www.whitehouse.gov/news/releases/2001/10/20011001-6.html.

55. George W. Bush, President Discusses Economic Recovery in New York City (2001 [cited August 2005]); available online at www.whitehouse.gov/news/releases/2001/10/20011003-4.html.

56. George W. Bush, President Unveils Back to Work Plan (2001 [cited August 2005]); available online at www.whitehouse.gov/news/releases/2001/10/20011004-8.html.

57. George W. Bush, President Bush and Italian Prime Minister Discuss War Effort (2001 [cited August 2005]); available online at www.whitehouse.gov/news/releases/2001/10/20011015-3.html.

58. *Washington Post*-ABC News Poll June 2005.

59. Mintz and Redd, "Framing Effects in International Relations."

60. H. Tajfel and J. C. Turner, "The Social Identity Theory of Intergroup Behaviour," in *Psychology of Intergroup Relations*, ed. S. Worchel and W. Austin (Chicago: Nelson-Hall, 1986).

61. Vaughn P. Shannon, "Norms Are What States Make of Them: The Political Psychology of Norm Violation," *International Studies Quarterly* 44, no. 2 (2000).

62. Bush, Address to a Joint Session of Congress and the American People.

63. George W. Bush, Statement by the President in His Address to the Nation (2001 [cited July 2005]); available online at www.whitehouse.gov/news/releases/2001/09/20010911-16.html.

64. Bush, President Urges Readiness and Patience.

65. Bush, President: FBI Needs Tools to Track Down Terrorists.

66. Bush, At O'Hare, President Says "Get on Board."

67. Bush, Address to a Joint Session of Congress and the American People.

68. George W. Bush, President, General Franks Discuss War Effort (2001 [cited July 2005]); available online at www.whitehouse.gov/news/releases/2001/12/20011228-1.html.

69. TIPP, *The Presidential Leadership Index* (TechnoMetrica Institute of Policy and Politics, 2001-2004 [cited August 2005]); available online at www.tipponline.com/n_index/pli/2004/pl_1204.htm, www.tipponline.com/n_index/pli/2003/pl_1203.htm, www.tipponline.com/n_index/eoi/eo_102.htm, *Pew Bush Leadership Approval Index*.

Chapter 5

1. Campbell and Jamieson, *Deeds Done in Words: Presidential Rhetoric and the Genres of Governance*.

2. Boettcher and Cobb, "Echoes of Vietnam?: Casualty Framing and Public Perceptions of Success and Failure in Iraq," Gelpi, Feaver, and Reifler, "Success Matters: Casualty Sensitivity and the War in Iraq," Christopher Gelpi and John Mueller, "The Cost of War," *Foreign Affairs*, January/February 2006.

3. Kahneman and Tversky, "Prospect Theory: An Analysis of Decision under Risk."

4. *Pew Bush Leadership Approval Index*.

5. "Unusually High Interest in Bush's State of the Union" Pew Research Center (2002).

6. Steven Kull, "Americans on the Conflict with Iraq," Program on International Policy Attitudes (PIPA/Knowledge Networks), Center on Policy Attitudes and the Center for International and Security Studies at Maryland (2002).

7. Dueck, "Ideas and Alternatives in American Grand Strategy, 2000–2004."

8. George W. Bush, President Delivers State of the Union Address (2002 [cited November 2005]); available online at www.whitehouse.gov/news/releases/2002/01/20020129-11.html.

9. Ibid.

10. Ibid.

11. Ibid.

12. Ibid.

13. Levin, Schneider, and Gaeth, "All Frames Are Not Created Equal: A Typology and Critical Analysis of Framing Effects."

14. Geva, Astorino-Courtois, and Mintz, "Marketing the Peace Process in the Middle East: The Effectiveness of Thematic and Evaluative Framing in Jordan and Israel."

15. Bush, President Delivers State of the Union Address.

16. Ibid.

17. Ibid.

18. Ibid.

19. Kean et al., "The Final Report of the National Commission on Terrorist Attacks upon the United States."

20. Bush, President Delivers State of the Union Address.

21. Ibid.

22. Ibid.

23. Ibid.

24. Ibid.

25. Ibid.

26. Ibid.

27. George W. Bush, President Bush Outlines Iraqi Threat (2002 [cited December 2005]); available online at www.whitehouse.gov/news/releases/2002/10/20021007-8.html.

28. Bush, President Delivers State of the Union Address.

29. Ibid.

30. Bush, President Stresses Volunteerism at Atlanta High School.

31. George W. Bush, President Outlines Education Reform in Boston Speech (2002 [cited November 2005]); available online at www.whitehouse.gov/news/releases/2002/01/20020108-5.html.

32. George W. Bush, President Bush, Prime Minister Blair Hold Press Conference (2002 [cited November 2005]); available online at http://www.whitehouse.gov/news/releases/2002/04/20020406-3.html.

33. George W. Bush, Remarks by the President at Anne Northup for Congress Luncheon (2002 [cited November 2005]); available online at www.whitehouse.gov/news/releases/2002/09/20020905-5.html.

34. George W. Bush, Remarks by the President at Republican Governors Association Fall Reception (2002 [cited November 2005]); available online at www.whitehouse.gov/news/releases/2002/09/20020919-14.html.

35. Ibid.

36. George W. Bush, President Focuses on Economy and War on Terrorism in Kentucky Speech (2002 [cited November 2005]); available online at www.whitehouse.gov/news/releases/2002/09/20020905-4.html.

37. George W. Bush, Remarks by the President at West Virginia Welcome (2002 [cited November 2005]); available online at www.whitehouse.gov/news/releases/2002/10/20021031-8.html.

38. George W. Bush, President Discusses Foreign Policy with Congressional Leaders (2002 [cited November 2005]); available online at www.whitehouse.gov/news/releases/2002/09/20020904-1.html.

39. George W. Bush, President Bush, Prime Minister Blair Discuss Keeping the Peace (2002 [cited November 2005]); available online at www.whitehouse.gov/news/releases/2002/09/20020907-2.html.

40. Bush, President Bush Outlines Iraqi Threat.

41. Ibid.

42. Ibid.

43. Ibid.

44. Ibid.

45. Ibid.

46. Ibid.

47. Ibid.

48. Ibid.

49. Ibid.

50. Ibid.

51. Ibid.

52. Ibid.

53. Ibid.

54. Ibid.

55. Ibid.

56. Ibid.

57. Ibid.

58. Ibid.

59. Ibid.

60. Ibid.

61. *Americans Thinking about Iraq, but Focused on the Economy,* Pew Research Center (2002 [cited December 2005]); available online at people-press.org/reports/display.php3?PageID=644.

62. Pew Bush Leadership Approval Index,. *TIPP, The Presidential Leadership Index.*

63. *Americans Thinking about Iraq, but Focused on the Economy.*

64. Would You Favor or Oppose Having U.S. Forces Take Military Action against Iraq to Force Saddam Hussein from Power? (Fieldwork by TNS Intersearch, 2003 [cited August 2005]); available online at www.pollingreport.com/iraq9.htm.

65. Do You Think Iraq Poses a Threat to the Us? ABC News Poll (Fieldwork by TNS Intersearch, 2003 [cited August 2005]); available online at www.pollingreport.com/iraq9.htm.

66. Americans Thinking about Iraq, but Focused on the Economy.

67. Steven Kull, "Public Opposes Congress Giving President Authority to Attack Iraq without UN Approval," Program on International Policy Attitudes (PIPA/Knowledge Networks), Center on Policy Attitudes and the Center for International and Security Studies at Maryland (2002).

68. Americans Thinking about Iraq, but Focused on the Economy.

69. *Post-Blix: Public Favors Force in Iraq, But . . . U.S. Needs More International Backing,* Pew Research Center in association with Council on Foreign Relations (2003 [cited December 3, 2005]); available online at www.pewtrusts.com/pdf/vf_pew_research_international_backing.pdf.

70. George W. Bush, President Bush: "World Can Rise to This Moment" (2003 [cited December 2005]); available online at www.whitehouse.gov/news/releases/2003/02/20030206-17.html.

71. Ibid.

72. George W. Bush, President Bush Discusses Faith-Based Initiative in Tennessee (2003 [cited December 2005]); available online at www.whitehouse.gov/news/releases/2003/02/20030210-1.html.

73. Bush, President Bush: "World Can Rise to This Moment."

74. George W. Bush, President Speaks at FBI on New Terrorist Threat Integration Center (2003 [cited December 2005]); available online at www.whitehouse.gov/news/releases/2003/02/20030214-5.html.

75. Ibid.

76. Bush, President Bush: "World Can Rise to This Moment."

77. Ibid.

78. George W. Bush, President Bush Meets with Prime Minister Howard of Australia (2003 [cited December 2005]); available online at www.whitehouse.gov/news/releases/2003/02/20030210-10.html.

79. George W. Bush, President Meets with National Economic Council (2003 [cited December 2005]); available online at www.whitehouse.gov/news/releases/2003/02/20030225-6.html.

80. George W. Bush, President Discusses the Future of Iraq (2003 [cited December 2005]); available online at www.whitehouse.gov/news/releases/2003/02/20030226-11.html.

81. This lack of thorough support for preemptive war among both Republicans and Democrats is proving to be the Achilles heel for the president's Iraq policy. At time of writing, most presidential candidates have been faced with the withdraw from Iraq issue and a majority of Americans favor a troop decline. *Solid Majority Favors Congressional Troop Deadline*, Pew Research Center (2007 [cited July 5, 2007]); available online at people-press.org/reports/pdf/313.pdf.

82. Pew Bush Leadership Approval Index.

83. Would You Favor or Oppose Having U.S. Forces Take Military Action against Iraq to Force Saddam Hussein from Power?.

84. Post-Blix: Public Favors Force in Iraq, But . . . U.S. Needs More International Backing.

85. National Strategy for Victory in Iraq, The White House (2005 [cited January 2006]); available online at www.whitehouse.gov/infocus/iraq/iraq_strategy_nov2005.html.

86. Gelpi, Feaver, and Reifler, "Success Matters: Casualty Sensitivity and the War in Iraq."

Chapter 6

1. Steven Kull, "Americans on Iraq: Wmd, Links to Al-Qaeda, Reconstruction," Program on International Policy Attitudes (PIPA/Knowledge Networks). Center on Policy Attitudes and the Center for International and Security Studies at Maryland (2003).

2. Ibid.

3. *Do You Think the U.S. Made the Right Decision or the Wrong Decision in Using Military Force against Iraq?*, Pew Research Center for the People and the Press survey, (2006 [cited January 2006]); available online at www.pollingreport.com/iraq.htm.

4. Investor's Business Daily/Christian Science Monitor/TIPP poll conducted by TechnoMetrica Market Intelligence. N = approx. 1000 adults nationwide. Available online at www.pollingreport.com/iraq4.htm.

5. CNN/*USA Today*/Gallup Poll, Nov. 11–13, 2005. Adults nationwide. Available online at www.pollingreport.com/iraq2.htm.

6. George W. Bush, President Bush Signs Homeland Security Appropriations Bill (2003 [cited August 2005]); available online at www.whitehouse.gov/news/releases/2003/10/20031001-4.html.

7. George W. Bush, Remarks by the President at Bush-Cheney 2004 Luncheon (2003 [cited August 2005]); available online at www.whitehouse.gov/news/releases/2003/10/20031003-6.html, George W. Bush, Remarks by the President at Bush-Cheney 2004 Reception (2003 [cited August 2005]); available online at www.whitehouse.gov/news/releases/2003/10/20031030-10.html.

8. Bush, Remarks by the President at Bush-Cheney 2004 Luncheon.

9. Bush, Remarks by the President at Bush-Cheney 2004 Reception.

10. George W. Bush, President Addresses Top Priorities: Economic and National Security (2003 [cited August 2005]); available online at www.whitehouse.gov/news/releases/2003/10/20031009-9.html, George W. Bush, President Bush Discusses the Economy and the War on Terror (2003 [cited August 2005]); available online at www.whitehouse.gov/news/releases/2003/10/20031016-3.html.

11. *Washington Post*-ABC News Poll June 2005.

12. Nearly all terms and frames hit low points in December of each year, mainly due to a significant decrease in presidential speeches. These lows are discounted when looking at trends and patterns in presidential framing.

13. Do You Favor Keeping a Large Number of U.S. Troops in Iraq until There Is a Stable Government There or Bringing Most of Our Troops Home in the Next Year? Harris Poll (2005 [cited January 2006]); available online at www.pollingreport.com/iraq2.htm.

14. Gelpi and Mueller, "The Cost of War."

15. To capture any type of framing related to these terms, *Victor** and *Win** were used as wildcard search terms for variants on the words, i.e., victory, victories, victorious, winning, winners, etc.

16. For an in-depth discussion of counter framing see Mintz and Redd, "Framing Effects in International Relations."

17. The proximity search looked for the words *terror** and *peace** within five words of Iraq.

18. George W. Bush, Remarks by the President of the American Legion (2004 [cited August 2005]).

19. George W. Bush, Remarks by the President at Bush-Cheney Rally (2004 [cited August 2005]); available online at www.whitehouse.gov/news/releases/2004/08/20040804-7.html.

20. George W. Bush, President Speaks at VFW Convention (2004 [cited August 2005]); available online at www.whitehouse.gov/news/releases/2004/08/20040816-12.html.

21. Scott Shane, "Bush's Speech on Iraq Echoes Analyst's Voice," *New York Times*, December 4 2005.

22. *Washington Post*–ABC News Poll June 2005. For survey data see www.washingtonpost.com/wp-srv/politics/polls/postpoll050607.pdf.

23. TIPP, The Presidential Leadership Index.

24. Steven Kull, "U.S. Public Beliefs and Attitudes About Iraq," Program on International Policy Attitudes (PIPA/Knowledge Networks), Center on Policy Attitudes and the Center for International and Security Studies at Maryland (2004).

25. Ibid.

26. Ibid.

27. *Most Say Al Qaeda Is Weaker Than before 9/11. Iraq Support Steady in Face of Higher Casualties*, Pew Research Center (2004 [cited December 2005]); available online at www.pewtrusts.com/pdf/PRC_Sept04_Iraq.pdf.

28. George W. Bush, President's Remarks in Davenport, Iowa (2004 [cited August 2005]); available online at www.whitehouse.gov/news/releases/2004/08/20040804-5.html.

29. George W. Bush, President's Remarks at Panama City, Florida Rally (2004 [cited December 2005]); available online at www.whitehouse.gov/news/releases/2004/08/20040810-19.html.

30. Ibid.

31. George W. Bush, Remarks by the President at Farmington, New Mexico Rally (2004 [cited December 2005]); available online at www.whitehouse.gov/news/releases/2004/08/20040826-10.html.

32. George W. Bush, President's Remarks at Victory 2004 Rally in West Chester, Ohio (2004 [cited August 2005]); available online at www.whitehouse.gov/news/releases/2004/09/20040927-8.html.

33. Ibid.

34. Ibid.

35. George W. Bush, President Bush and Prime Minister Allawi Press Conference (2004 [cited August 2005]); available online at www.whitehouse.gov/news/releases/2004/09/20040923-8.html.

36. George W. Bush, Remarks by the President at Victory 2004 Rally (2004 [cited August 2005]); available from http://www.whitehouse.gov/news/releases/2004/10/20041001-15.html.

37. George W. Bush, President's Remarks at a Victory 2004 Rally in Farmington Hills, Michigan (2004 [cited August 2005]); available from http://www.whitehouse.gov/news/releases/2004/10/20041006-16.html.

38. Ibid.([cited).

39. Geva, Astorino-Courtois, and Mintz, "Marketing the Peace Process in the Middle East: The Effectiveness of Thematic and Evaluative Framing in Jordan and Israel," 362.

40. George W. Bush, Remarks by the President to the American Legion (2004 [cited August 2005]); available online at www.whitehouse.gov/news/releases/2004/08/20040831-7.html.

41. Bush, President's Remarks in Davenport, Iowa.

42. George W. Bush, President's Remarks at Ask President Bush Event (2004 [cited August 2005]); available online at www.whitehouse.gov/news/releases/2004/08/20040810-15.html.

43. George W. Bush, President's Remarks at Ask President Bush Event in Derry, New Hampshire (2004 [cited August 2005]); available online at www.whitehouse.gov/news/releases/2004/09/20040920-11.html.

44. Bush, President's Remarks at Ask President Bush Event.

45. Steven Kull, "Americans and Iraq on the Eve of the Presidential Election," Program on International Policy Attitudes (PIPA/Knowledge Networks), Center on Policy Attitudes and the Center for International and Security Studies at Maryland (2004).

46. Ibid.

47. George W. Bush, Remarks by President Bush and Senator Kerry in First 2004 Presidential Debate (2004 [cited August 2005]); available online at www.whitehouse.gov/news/releases/2004/10/20041001.html.

48. Ibid.

49. Ibid.

50. Ibid.

51. Ibid.

52. George W. Bush, President's Remarks at an Ask President Bush Event in Clive, Iowa (2004 [cited August 2005]); available online at www.whitehouse.gov/news/releases/2004/10/20041004-12.html.

53. Bush, President's Remarks at a Victory 2004 Rally in Farmington Hills, Michigan.

54. Ibid.

55. *Familiar Divides, Post-Election Disengagement, Public Opinion Little Changed by Presidential Election*, Pew Research Center (2004 [cited August 2005]); available online at www.pewtrusts.com/pdf/PRC_postelec_1204.pdf.

56. *Neither Election nor Fighting in Fallujah Changes Public Attitudes on Iraq* (2004 [cited January 2006]); available online at www.harrisinteractive.com/harris_poll/index.asp?PID=522.

57. Robert L. Hutchings, *Mapping the Global Future* (National Intelligence Council, 2004 [cited January 2006]); available online at www.cia.gov/nic/NIC_globaltrend2020.html.

Chapter 7

1. *Washington Post*-ABC News Poll June 2005.

2. Overwhelming Support for Bush, Military Response But . . . American Psyche Reeling from Terror Attacks.

3. Gary King, Robert Keohane, and Sidney Verba, *Designing Social Inquiry: Scientific Inference in Qualitative Research* (Princeton, NJ: Princeton University Press, 1994), 185.

4. Terrance Odean, "Are Investors Reluctant to Realize Their Losses?," in *Choices, Values, and Frames*, ed. Daniel Kahneman and Amos Tversky (Cambridge: Cambridge University Press, 2000), Hersh Shefrin and Meir Statman, "The Disposition to Sell Winners Too Early and Ride Losers Too Long: Theory and Evidence," *Journal of Finance* 40, no. 3 (1985).

5. Robert J. Shiller, "Human Behavior and the Efficiency of the Financial System," in *Handbook of Macroeconomics*, ed. John B. Taylor and Michael Woodford (North-Holland, 1999).

6. *Modest Election Optimism, Positive Views of Iraqi Troop Training*, Pew Research Center (2005 [cited 2006]); available online at www.pewtrusts.com/pdf/PRC_Iraq_1205.pdf.

7. Ibid.

8. Kull, Americans on the War on Terrorism: A Study of US Public Attitudes.

9. Future research may examine whether or not public opinion spurred or limited the expansion of ongoing war aims. Additionally, domestic public opinion may have some correlation to a state's willingness to adequately launch a counter insurgency, i.e., France in Algeria, the United States in Southeast Asia, and the Soviet Union in Afghanistan. The operating assumption being that successful counterinsurgency operations require tactics

that exceed the public's norms of wartime behavior; see David Galula, *Counterinsurgency Warfare: Theory and Practice*, 2nd ed. (Praeger Security International, 2005).

10. Jentleson, "The Pretty Prudent Public: Post Post-Vietnam American Opinion on the Use of Military Force."

11. Jon Western, "Sources of Humanitarian Intervention," *International Security* 26, no. 4 (2002).

12. Mueller, *Policy and Opinion in the Gulf War*, xiv.

13. Kahneman and Tversky, "Prospect Theory: An Analysis of Decision under Risk," Quattrone and Tversky, "Contrasting Rational and Psychological Analyses of Political Choice."

14. See David Gergen, *Eyewitness to Power: The Essence of Leadership Nixon to Clinton* (New York: Simon and Schuster, 2000), Seymour Martin Lipset, *American Exceptionalism: A Double-Edged Sword* (New York: W. W. Norton, 1996).

15. Richard W. Stevenson, "President Makes It Clear: Phrase Is 'War on Terror'," *New York Times*, August 4, 2005.

16. Rove: Security Will Be Focus of 2006 Campaigns (CNN, 2006 [cited January 2006]); available online at www.cnn.com/2006/POLITICS/01/20/republicans.rove.ap/index.html.

Epilogue

1. George W. Bush, Press Conference by the President (2006 [cited June 30, 2007 2007]); available online at www.whitehouse.gov/news/releases/2006/12/20061220-1.html.

2. Lawrence Eagleburger et al., *Iraq Study Group Report,* USIP (December 2006 2006 [cited June 2007]); available online at www.usip.org/isg/iraq_study_group_report/report/1206/iraq_study_group_report.pdf.

3. George W. Bush, President Bush Participates in Briefings at U.S. Department of Defense (2007 [cited June 30, 2007]); available online at www.whitehouse.gov/news/releases/2007/05/20070510-6.html.

4. George W. Bush, President Bush Participates in Roundtable with Travel Pool (2007 [cited June 30, 2007]); available online at www.whitehouse.gov/news/releases/2007/06/20070606-10.html.

5. Shailagh Murray, "Clinton, Obama to Back Vote to Cut Off Funding for Troops in Iraq," *Washington Post* 2007.

6. Solid Majority Favors Congressional Troop Deadline.

7. John Whitesides, "Clinton's Iraq Vote Haunts Her on Campaign Trail" (Reuters, 2007 [cited June 30, 2007]); available online at www.reuters.com/article/topNews/idUSN2237058420070223.

8. Fred Barnes, "A McCain Surge? Defending the Iraq War Is His Best Shot," *Weekly Standard*, April 23, 2007.

9. Solid Majority Favors Congressional Troop Deadline.

10. Ibid.

Bibliography

Allison, Graham T., "Conceptual Models and the Cuban Missile Crisis," *American Political Science Review*, Vol. 63, No. 3 (1969).

Allison, Graham T, and Phillip Zelikow, *Essence of Decision: Explaining the Cuban Missile Crisis* (New York: Addison Wesley Longman, 1999).

Americans Thinking about Iraq, but Focused on the Economy. 2002. Pew Research Center, people-press.org/reports/display.php3?PageID=644 (accessed December 2005).

Andrade, Lydia, and Garry Young, "Presidential Agenda Setting: Influences on the Emphasis of Foreign Policy," *Political Research Quarterly*, Vol. 49, No. 3 (1996), 591–605.

Barberis, N., M. Huang, and T. Santos, "Prospect Theory and Asset Prices," *Quarterly Journal of Economics*, Vol. 116, No. 1 (2001), 1–53.

Barnes, Fred, "A McCain Surge? Defending the Iraq War Is His Best Shot," *Weekly Standard*, April 23, 2007.

Baumgartner, Frank R., and Bryan D. Jones, *Agendas and Instability in American Politics* (Chicago: University of Chicago Press, 1993).

———, "Representation and Agenda Setting," *Policy Studies Journal*, Vol. 32, No. 1 (2004), 1–24.

Bayoumi, A. M., and D. A. Redelmeier, "Decision Analysis with Cumulative Prospect Theory," *Medical Decision Making*, Vol. 20, No. 4 (2000), 404–412.

Behr, Roy L., and Shanto Iyengar, "Television News, Real-World Cues, and Changes in the Public Agenda," *Public Opinion Quarterly*, Vol. 49, No. 1 (1985), pp. 38–57.

Boettcher, William A., "The Prospects for Prospect Theory: An Empirical Evaluation of International Relations Applications of Framing and Loss Aversion," *Political Psychology*, Vol. 25, No. 3 (2004), pp. 331–362.

Boettcher, William A., and Michael D. Cobb, "Echoes of Vietnam?: Casualty Framing and Public Perceptions of Success and Failure in Iraq," *Journal of Conflict Resolution*, Vol. 50 (2006), 831–854.

Boettcher, William A. III, "Context, Methods, Numbers, and Words: Prospect Theory in International Relations," *Journal of Conflict Resolution*, Vol. 39, No. 3 (1995), 561–583.

Boettcher, William A. III, "Military Intervention Decisions Regarding Humanitarian Crises: Framing Induced Risk Behavior," *Journal of Conflict Resolution*, Vol. 48, No. 3 (2004), 331–355.

Bueno de Mesquita, Bruce, *Principles of International Politics: People's Power, Preferences and Perceptions* (Washington, DC: CQ Press, 2000).

Bueno de Mesquita, Bruce, Alastair Smith, Randolph M. Siverson, and James D. Morrow, *The Logic of Political Survival* (Cambridge, MA: MIT Press, 2003).

Bush, George W., Address to a Joint Session of Congress and the American People, 2001, www.whitehouse.gov/news/releases/2001/09/20010920-8.html (accessed August 2005).

———, At O'Hare, President Says "Get on Board," 2001, www.whitehouse.gov/news/releases/2001/09/20010927-1.html (accessed July 2005).

———, President Addresses Top Priorities: Economic & National Security, 2003, www.whitehouse.gov/news/releases/2003/10/20031009-9.html (accessed August 2005).

———, President Bush and Italian Prime Minister Discuss War Effort, 2001, www.whitehouse.gov/news/releases/2001/10/20011015-3.html. (accessed August 2005).

———, President Bush and Prime Minister Allawi Press Conference, 2004, www.whitehouse.gov/news/releases/2004/09/20040923-8.html (accessed August 2005).

———, President Bush Discusses Faith-Based Initiative in Tennessee, 2003, http://www.whitehouse.gov/news/releases/2003/02/20030210-1.html (accessed December 2005).

———, President Bush Discusses the Economy and the War on Terror, 2003, www.whitehouse.gov/news/releases/2003/10/20031016-3.html (accessed August 2005).

———, President Bush Meets with Prime Minister Howard of Australia, 2003, www.whitehouse.gov/news/releases/2003/02/20030210-10.html (accessed December 2005).

———, President Bush Outlines Iraqi Threat, 2002, www.whitehouse.gov/news/releases/2002/10/20021007-8.html (accessed December 2005).

———, President Bush Participates in Briefings at U.S. Department of Defense, 2007, www.whitehouse.gov/news/releases/2007/05/20070510-6.html (accessed June 30, 2007).

———, President Bush Participates in Roundtable with Travel Pool, 2007, www.whitehouse.gov/news/releases/2007/06/20070606-10.html (accessed June 30, 2007).

———, President Bush Salutes Heroes in New York, 2001, www.whitehouse.gov/news/releases/2001/09/20010914-9.html (accessed July 2005).

———, President Bush Signs Homeland Security Appropriations Bill, 2003, www.whitehouse.gov/news/releases/2003/10/20031001-4.html (accessed August 2005).

———, President Bush, Prime Minister Blair Discuss Keeping the Peace, 2002, www.whitehouse.gov/news/releases/2002/09/20020907-2.html (accessed November 2005).

———, President Bush, Prime Minister Blair Hold Press Conference, 2002, www.whitehouse.gov/news/releases/2002/04/20020406-3.html (accessed November 2005).

———, President Bush: "World Can Rise to This Moment," 2003, www.whitehouse.gov/news/releases/2003/02/20030206-17.html (accessed December 2005).

———, President Delivers State of the Union Address, 2002, www.whitehouse.gov/news/releases/2002/01/20020129-11.html (accessed November 2005).

———, President Discusses Economic Recovery in New York City, 2001, www.whitehouse.gov/news/releases/2001/10/20011003-4.html (accessed August 2005).

———, President Discusses Foreign Policy with Congressional Leaders, 2002, www.whitehouse.gov/news/releases/2002/09/20020904-1.html (accessed November 2005).

———, President Discusses the Future of Iraq, 2003, www.whitehouse.gov/news/releases/2003/02/20030226-11.html (accessed December 2005).

————, President Focuses on Economy and War on Terrorism in Kentucky Speech, 2002, www.whitehouse.gov/news/releases/2002/09/20020905-4.html (accessed November 2005).

————, President George W. Bush's Inaugural Address, 2001, www.whitehouse.gov/news/inaugural-address.html (accessed August 2005).

————, President Holds Prime Time News Conference, 2001, www.whitehouse.gov/news/releases/2001/10/20011011-7.html# (accessed August 2005).

————, President Holds Town Hall Forum on Economy in California, 2002 www.whitehouse.gov/news/releases/2002/01/20020105-3.html (accessed August 2005).

————, President Launches Online American Relief and Response Effort, 2001, www.whitehouse.gov/news/releases/2001/09/20010918-1.html (accessed July 2005).

————, President Meets with Economic Advisors and Federal Reserve Chairman Greenspan, 2002, www.whitehouse.gov/news/releases/2002/01/20020107-3.html (accessed August 2005).

————, President Meets with National Economic Council, 2003, www.whitehouse.gov/news/releases/2003/02/20030225-6.html (accessed December 2005).

————, President Outlines Education Reform in Boston Speech, 2002, www.whitehouse.gov/news/releases/2002/01/20020108-5.html (accessed November 2005).

————, President Reports Progress, Calls for Action in Cabinet Meeting, 2001, www.whitehouse.gov/news/releases/2001/10/20011011-3.html (accessed July 2005).

————, President Speaks at FBI on New Terrorist Threat Integration Center, 2003, www.whitehouse.gov/news/releases/2003/02/20030214-5.html (accessed December 2005).

————, President Speaks at VFW Convention, 2004, www.whitehouse.gov/news/releases/2004/08/20040816-12.html (accessed August 2005).

————, President Stresses Volunteerism at Atlanta High School, 2002, www.whitehouse.gov/news/releases/2002/01/20020131-7.html (accessed August 2005).

————, President Thanks CIA, 2001, www.whitehouse.gov/news/releases/2001/09/20010926-3.html (accessed July 2005).

————, President Unveils "Most Wanted" Terrorists, 2001, www.whitehouse.gov/news/releases/2001/10/20011010-3.html (accessed August 2005).

————, President Unveils Back to Work Plan, 2001, www.whitehouse.gov/news/releases/2001/10/20011004-8.html (accessed August 2005).

————, President Urges Action on Economic Plan to Oregon Workers, 2002, www.whitehouse.gov/news/releases/2002/01/20020105-6.html (accessed August, 2005).

————, President Urges Readiness and Patience, 2001, www.whitehouse.gov/news/releases/2001/09/20010915-4.html (accessed July 2005).

————, President, General Franks Discuss War Effort, 2001, www.whitehouse.gov/news/releases/2001/12/20011228-1.html (accessed July 2005).

————, President: "We're Making Progress," 2001, www.whitehouse.gov/news/releases/2001/10/20011001-6.html (accessed July 2005).

————, President: FBI Needs Tools to Track Down Terrorists, 2001, www.whitehouse.gov/news/releases/2001/09/20010925-5.html (accessed July 2005).

————, Presidential Address to the Nation, 2001, www.whitehouse.gov/news/releases/2001/10/20011007-8.html (accessed August 2005).

————, President's Remarks at a Victory 2004 Rally in Farmington Hills, Michigan, 2004, www.whitehouse.gov/news/releases/2004/10/20041006-16.html (accessed August 2005).

Bush, George W., President's Remarks at an Ask President Bush Event in Clive, Iowa, 2004, www.whitehouse.gov/news/releases/2004/10/20041004-12.html (accessed August 2005).

———, President's Remarks at Ask President Bush Event, 2004, www.whitehouse.gov/news/releases/2004/08/20040810-15.html (accessed August 2005).

———, President's Remarks at Ask President Bush Event in Derry, New Hampshire, 2004, www.whitehouse.gov/news/releases/2004/09/20040920-11.html (accessed August 2005).

———, President's Remarks at National Day of Prayer and Remembrance, 2001, www.whitehouse.gov/news/releases/2001/09/20010914-2.html (accessed August 2005).

———, President's Remarks at Panama City, Florida Rally, 2004, www.whitehouse.gov/news/releases/2004/08/20040810-19.html (accessed December 2005).

———, President's Remarks at Victory 2004 Rally in West Chester, Ohio, 2004, www.whitehouse.gov/news/releases/2004/09/20040927-8.html (accessed August 2005).

———, President's Remarks in Davenport, Iowa, 2004, www.whitehouse.gov/news/releases/2004/08/20040804-5.html (accessed August 2005).

———, Press Conference by the President, 2006, www.whitehouse.gov/news/releases/2006/12/20061220-1.html (accessed June 30, 2007).

———, Remarks by President Bush and Senator Kerry in First 2004 Presidential Debate, 2004, www.whitehouse.gov/news/releases/2004/10/20041001.html (accessed August 2005).

———, Remarks by the President at Anne Northup for Congress Luncheon, 2002, www.whitehouse.gov/news/releases/2002/09/20020905-5.html (accessed November 2005).

———, Remarks by the President at Bush-Cheney 2004 Luncheon, 2003, www.whitehouse.gov/news/releases/2003/10/20031003-6.html (accessed August 2005).

———, Remarks by the President at Bush-Cheney 2004 Reception, 2003, www.whitehouse.gov/news/releases/2003/10/20031030-10.html (accessed August 2005).

———, Remarks by the President at Bush-Cheney Rally, 2004, www.whitehouse.gov/news/releases/2004/08/20040804-7.html (accessed August 2005).

———, Remarks by the President at Camp Pendleton, California, 2001, www.whitehouse.gov/news/releases/2001/05/20010529-6.html (accessed August 2005).

———, Remarks by the President at Farmington, New Mexico Rally, 2004, www.whitehouse.gov/news/releases/2004/08/20040826-10.html (accessed December, 2005).

———, Remarks by the President at Memorial Day Commemoration, 2001, www.whitehouse.gov/news/releases/2001/05/20010529-1.html (accessed August 2005).

———, Remarks by the President at Photo Opportunity with House and Senate Leadership, 2001, www.whitehouse.gov/news/releases/2001/09/20010919-8.html (accessed July 2005).

———, Remarks by the President at Republican Governors Association Fall Reception, 2002, www.whitehouse.gov/news/releases/2002/09/20020919-14.html (accessed November 2005).

———, Remarks by the President at U.S. Naval Academy Commencement, 2001, www.whitehouse.gov/news/releases/2001/05/20010525-1.html (accessed August 2005).

———, Remarks by the President at Victory 2004 Rally, 2004, www.whitehouse.gov/news/releases/2004/10/20041001-15.html (accessed August 2005).

———, Remarks by the President at West Virginia Welcome, 2002, www.whitehouse.gov/news/releases/2002/10/20021031-8.html (accessed November 2005).

———, Remarks by the President to the American Legion, 2004 (accessed August 2005).

————, Remarks by the President to National Guard Personnel, 2001, www.whitehouse .gov/news/releases/2001/02/20010214-2.html (accessed August 2005).

————, Remarks by the President to Southwest Michigan First Coalition/Kalamazoo Chamber of Commerce Joint Event on the Economy, 2001, www.whitehouse.gov/ news/releases/2001/03/20010327-5.html (accessed August 2005).

————, Remarks by the President to State Department Employees, 2001, www .whitehouse.gov/news/releases/2001/02/20010215-5.html (accessed August 2005).

————, Remarks by the President to Students and Faculty at National Defense University, 2001, www.whitehouse.gov/news/releases/2001/05/20010501-10.html (accessed August 2005).

————, Remarks by the President to the American Legion, 2004, www.whitehouse.gov/ news/releases/2004/08/20040831-7.html (accessed August 2005).

————, Remarks by the President to the Greater Portland Chambers of Commerce Meeting, 2001, www.whitehouse.gov/news/releases/2001/03/20010323.html (accessed August 2005).

————, Remarks by the President upon Arrival, 2001, www.whitehouse.gov/news/ releases/2001/09/20010916-2.html (accessed July 2005).

————, Statement by the President in His Address to the Nation, 2001, www.whitehouse .gov/news/releases/2001/09/20010911-16.html (accessed July 2005).

————, Statement by the President: Domestic Preparedness against Weapons of Mass Destruction, 2001, www.whitehouse.gov/news/releases/2001/05/20010508.html (accessed August 2005).

Cameron, Charles, John S. Lapinski, and Charles R. Riemann, "Testing Formal Theories of Political Rhetoric," *Journal of Politics*, Vol. 62, No. 1 (2000), 187–205.

Campbell, Karlyn Kohrs, and Kathleen Hall Jamieson, *Deeds Done in Words: Presidential Rhetoric and the Genres of Governance* (Chicago: University of Chicago Press, 1990).

Carmines, Edward G., and Richard A. Zeller, eds., *Reliability and Validity Assessment* (Sage Publications, 1979).

Chilton, Paul, *Analysing Political Discourse Theory and Practice* (London: Routledge, 2004).

Christensen, Thomas J., *Useful Adversaries: Grand Strategy, Domestic Mobilization, and Sino-American Conflict, 1947–1958* (Princeton, NJ: Princeton University Press, 1996).

Cioffi-Revilla, Claudio, *Politics and Uncertainty: Theory and Applications* (New York: Cambridge University Press, 1998).

Cohen, Jeffrey E., "Presidential Rhetoric and the Public Agenda," *American Journal of Political Science*, Vol. 39, No. 1 (1995), 87–107.

Dedaic, Mirjana N., and Daniel N. Nelson, *At War with Words* (New York: Mouton de Gruyter, 2003).

Do You Favor Keeping a Large Number of U.S. Troops in Iraq until There Is a Stable Government There or Bringing Most of Our Troops Home in the Next Year?, 2005, Harris Poll, www.pollingreport.com/iraq2.htm (accessed January 2006).

Do You Think Iraq Poses a Threat to the US? ABC News Poll, 2003, Fieldwork by TNS Intersearch, www.pollingreport.com/iraq9.htm (accessed August 2005).

Do You Think the U.S. Made the Right Decision or the Wrong Decision in Using Military Force against Iraq?, 2006, Pew Research Center for the People and the Press survey, www.pollingreport.com/iraq.htm (accessed January 2006).

Dueck, Colin, "Ideas and Alternatives in American Grand Strategy, 2000–2004," *Review of International Studies*, Vol. 30 (2004), 511–535.

Economy, Education, Social Security Dominate Public's Policy Agenda, 2001, Pew Research Center, people-press.org/reports/display.php3?ReportID=4 (accessed August 2005).

Edwards, Adrian, Glyn Elwyn, Judith Covey, Elaine Matthews, and Roisin Pill, "Presenting Risk Information—A Review of the Effects of 'Framing' and Other Manipulations on Patient Outcomes," *Journal of Health Communication*, Vol. 6, No. 1 (2001), 61–82.

Familiar Divides, Post-Election Disengagement, Public Opinion Little Changed by Presidential Election, 2004, Pew Research Center, www.pewtrusts.com/pdf/PRC_postelec_1204.pdf (accessed August 2005).

Fanis, Maria, "Collective Action Meets Prospect Theory: An Application to Coalition Building in Chile, 1973–75," *Political Psychology*, Vol. 25, No. 3 (2004), 363–388.

Farnham, Barbara, "Roosevelt and the Munich Crisis—Insights from Prospect Theory," *Political Psychology*, Vol. 13, No. 2 (1992), 205–235.

Feaver, Peter, and Christopher Gelpi, *Choosing Your Battles: American Civil-Military Relations and the Use of Force* (Princeton, NJ: Princeton University Press, 2004).

Feldman, Stanley, ed., *Answering Survey Questions: The Measurement and Meaning of Public Opinion* (Ann Arbor: University of Michigan Press, 1995).

Fennema, H., and P. Wakker, "Original and Cumulative Prospect Theory: A Discussion of Empirical Differences," *Journal of Behavioral Decision Making*, Vol. 10, No. 1 (1997), 53–64.

Friedman, M., *A Theory of the Consumption Function* (Princeton, NJ: Princeton University Press, 1957).

Galula, David, *Counterinsurgency Warfare: Theory and Practice* (Praeger Security International, 2005).

Gaubatz, Kurt Taylor, *Elections and War: The Electoral Incentive in the Democratic Politics of War and Peace* (Stanford, CA: Stanford University Press, 1999).

Gelderman, Carol, *All the President's Words* (New York: Walker, 1997).

Gelpi, Christopher, Peter Feaver, and Jason Reifler, "Success Matters: Casualty Sensitivity and the War in Iraq," *Journal of International Security* (Winter 2005/2006).

Gelpi, Christopher, and John Mueller, "The Cost of War," *Foreign Affairs* (January/February 2006).

Gergen, David, *Eyewitness to Power: The Essence of Leadership Nixon to Clinton* (New York: Simon and Schuster, 2000).

Geva, Nehemia, Allison Astorino-Courtois, and Alex Mintz, "Marketing the Peace Process in the Middle East: The Effectiveness of Thematic and Evaluative Framing in Jordan and Israel," in Manas Chatterji, Jacques Fontanel and Akira Hattori, eds., *Arms Spending, Development and Security* (New Delhi: APH Publishing, 1996).

Gilpin, Robert, *War and Change in World Politics* (Cambridge: Cambridge University Press, 1981).

Green, Donald P., and Ian Shapiro, *Pathologies of Rational Choice: A Critique of Applications in Political Science* (New Haven, CT: Yale University Press, 1994).

Holsti, Ole R., *Content Analysis for the Social Sciences and Humanities* (Reading, MA: Addison-Wesley, 1969).

Hutchings, Robert L., Mapping the Global Future, 2004, National Intelligence Council, www.cia.gov/nic/NIC_globaltrend2020.html (accessed January 2006).

Iyengar, Shanto, "How Citizens Think about National Issues: A Matter of Responsibility," *American Journal of Political Science*, Vol. 33, No. 4 (1989), 878–900.

Jentleson, Bruce W., "The Pretty Prudent Public: Post Post-Vietnam American Opinion on the Use of Military Force," *International Studies Quarterly*, Vol. 36 (1992), 49–74.

Jervis, Robert, "Political Implications of Loss Aversion," *Political Psychology*, Vol. 13, No. 2 (1992), 187–204.

Kahler, Miles, "Rationality in International Relations," *International Organization*, Vol. 52, No. 4, International Organization at Fifty: Exploration and Contestation in the Study of World Politics (1998), 919–941.

Kahneman, Daniel, and Amos Tversky, "Choices, Values and Frames," *American Psychologist*, Vol. 39 (1984), 341–350.

———, "Choices, Values, and Frames," in Daniel Kahneman and Amos Tversky, eds., *Choices, Values, and Frames* (Cambridge: Cambridge University Press, 2000).

———, "Prospect Theory: An Analysis of Decision under Risk," *Econometrica: Journal of the Econometric Society*, Vol. 47, No. 2 (1979), 263–292.

Kapstein, Ethan, "Is Realism Dead? The Domestic Sources of International Politics," *International Organization*, Vol. 49 (1995), 751–774.

Kean, Thomas H., Lee H. Hamilton, Richard Ben-Veniste, Fred F. Fielding, Jamie S. Gorelick, Slade Gorton, Bob Kerrey, John F. Lehman, Timothy J. Roemer, and James R. Thompson, *The Final Report of the National Commission on Terrorist Attacks upon the United States*, 2004.

King, Gary, Robert Keohane, and Sidney Verba, *Designing Social Inquiry: Scientific Inference in Qualitative Research* (Princeton, NJ: Princeton University Press, 1994).

Kingdon, John W., *Agendas, Alternatives, and Public Policies* (Boston: Little Brown, 1995).

Kipfer, Barbara Ann, ed., *Roget's New Millennium* Thesaurus (Lexico Publishing Group, 2005).

Knapp, P., D. K. Raynor, and D. C. Berry, "Comparison of Two Methods of Presenting Risk Information to Patients About the Side Effects of Medicines," *Quality and Safety in Health Care*, Vol. 13, No. 3 (2004), 176–180.

Kull, Steven, *Americans and Iraq on the Eve of the Presidential Election*, 2004, Program on International Policy Attitudes (PIPA/Knowledge Networks). Center on Policy Attitudes and the Center for International and Security Studies at Maryland.

———, *Americans on Iraq: Wmd, Links to Al-Qaeda, Reconstruction*, 2003, Program on International Policy Attitudes (PIPA/Knowledge Networks). Center on Policy Attitudes and the Center for International and Security Studies at Maryland.

———, *Americans on the Conflict with Iraq*, 2002, Program on International Policy Attitudes (PIPA/Knowledge Networks). Center on Policy Attitudes and the Center for International and Security Studies at Maryland.

———, *Americans on the War on Terrorism: A Study of US Public Attitudes*, 2001, Program on International Policy Attitudes, www.pipa.org/OnlineReports/Terrorism/WarOnTerror_Nov01/WarOnTerror_Nov01_rpt.pdf (accessed August 2005).

———, *Public Opposes Congress Giving President Authority to Attack Iraq without UN Approval*, 2002, Program on International Policy Attitudes (PIPA/Knowledge Networks). Center on Policy Attitudes and the Center for International and Security Studies at Maryland.

———, *U.S. Public Beliefs and Attitudes about Iraq*, 2004, Program on International Policy Attitudes (PIPA/Knowledge Networks). Center on Policy Attitudes and the Center for International and Security Studies at Maryland.

Kull, Steven, and I. M. Destler, *Misreading the Public: The Myth of a New Isolationism* (Washington, DC: Brookings Institution Press, 1999).

Larson, Eric V., *Casualties and Consensus: The Historical Role of Casualties in Domestic Support for U.S. Military Operations* (Santa Monica, CA: RAND Corporation, 1996).

Lavoy, Peter, "What's New in the New U.S. Strategy to Combat Wmd?," *Strategic Insights*, Vol. I, No. 10 (2002).

Lawrence Eagleburger, et al., *Iraq Study Group Report*, 2006, USIP, www.usip.org/isg/iraq_study_group_report/report/1206/iraq_study_group_report.pdf (accessed June 2007).

Levin, Irwin P., Sandra L. Schneider, and Gary J. Gaeth, "All Frames Are Not Created Equal: A Typology and Critical Analysis of Framing Effects," *Organizational Behavior and Human Decision Processes*, Vol. 76, No. 2 (1998), 149–188.

Levy, Jack S., "An Introduction to Prospect Theory," *Political Psychology*, Vol. 13, No. 2 (1992), 171–186.

———, "Prospect Theory and International Relations—Theoretical Applications and Analytical Problems," *Political Psychology*, Vol. 13, No. 2 (1992), 283–310.

Light, Paul C., *The President's Agenda: Domestic Policy Choice from Kennedy to Carter* (Baltimore, MD: Johns Hopkins University Press, 1982).

Lipset, Seymour Martin, *American Exceptionalism: A Double-Edged Sword* (New York: W. W. Norton, 1996).

List, J. A., "Neoclassical Theory versus Prospect Theory: Evidence from the Marketplace," *Econometrica*, Vol. 72, No. 2 (2004), 615–625.

Lopes, Lola L., and Gregg C. Oden, "The Role of Aspiration Level in Risky Choice: A Comparison of Cumulative Prospect Theory and Sp/a Theory," *Journal of Mathematical Psychology*, Vol. 43, No. 2 (1999), 286–313.

Mandel, David R., "Gain-Loss Framing and Choice: Separating Outcome Formulations from Descriptor Formulations," *Organizational Behavior and Human Decision Processes*, Vol. 85, No. 1 (2001), 56–76.

March, James G., *A Primer on Decision Making: How Decisions Happen* (New York: Free Press, 1994).

March, James G., and Simon A. Herbert, *Organizations* (Cambridge, MA: Blackwell Publishers, 1993).

Marshall, Grant N., Lois M. Davis, and Cathy D. Sherbourne. *A Review of the Scientific Literature as It Pertains to Gulf War Illnesses*, 2000, www.rand.org/pubs/monograph_reports/MR1018.4-1 (accessed 2006).

McDermott, Rose, "Prospect Theory in Political Science: Gains and Losses from the First Decade," *Political Psychology*, Vol. 25, No. 2 (2004), 289–312.

———, "Prospect-Theory in International-Relations—The Iranian Hostage Rescue Mission," *Political Psychology*, Vol. 13, No. 2 (1992), 237–263.

———, *Risk-Taking in International Politics: Prospect Theory in American Foreign Policy* (Ann Arbor: University of Michigan Press, 1998).

Mercer, Jonathan, "Rationality and Psychology in International Politics," *International Organization*, Vol. 59, Winter (2005), 77–106.

Military News: Defense Policy/Programs, 2003, www.globalsecurity.org/military/library/news/2003/01/01-03_index.htm#policy (accessed February 2006).

Milliken, Jennifer, "The Study of Discourse in International Relations: A Critique of Research and Methods," *European Journal of International Relations*, Vol. 5, No. 2 (1999), 225–254.

Milner, Helen V., *Interests, Institutions, and Information: Domestic Politics and International Relations* (Princeton, NJ: Princeton University Press, 1997).

Mintz, A., and S. B. Redd, "Framing Effects in International Relations," *Synthese*, Vol. 135, No. 2 (2003), 193–213.

Mintz, Alex, "Foreign Policy Decisionmaking: Bridging the Gap between the Cognitive Psychology and Rational Actor 'Schools'," in Nehemia Geva and Alex Mintz., ed., *Decisionmaking on War and Peace: The Cognitive-Rational Debate* (Boulder, CO: Lynne Rienner Publishers, 1997).

Modest Election Optimism, Positive Views of Iraqi Troop Training, 2005, Pew Research Center, www.pewtrusts.com/pdf/PRC_Iraq_1205.pdf (accessed 2006).

Moeller, Susan D., *Media Coverage of Weapons of Mass Destruction*, 2004,, Center for International and Security Studies at Maryland, www.cissm.umd.edu/documents/WMDstudy_full.pdf (accessed 2005).

Moore, Will H., and David J. Lanoue, "Domestic Politics and U.S. Foreign Policy: A Study of Cold War Conflict Behavior," *Journal of Politics*, Vol. 65, No. 2 (2003), 376–396.

Moravcsik, Andrew, "Taking Preferences Seriously: A Liberal Theory of International Politics," *International Organization*, Vol. 51, No. 4 (1997), 513–553.

Morrow, James D., "Bargaining in Repeated Crises: A Limited Information Model," in Peter C. Ordeshook, ed., *Models of Strategic Choice in Politics* (Ann Arbor: University of Michigan Press, 1989).

———, "A Rational Choice Approach to International Conflict," in Nehemia Geva and Alex Mintz., ed., *Decision Making on War and Peace: The Cognitive-Rational Debate* (Boulder, CO: Lynne Rienner Publishers, 1997).

Most, Benjamin A., and Harvey Starr, *Inquiry, Logic and International Politics* (Columbia: University of South Carolina, 1989).

Most Say Al Qaeda Is Weaker Than before 9/11, Iraq Support Steady in Face of Higher Casualties,2004, Pew Research Center, www.pewtrusts.com/pdf/PRC_Sept04_Iraq. pdf (accessed December 2005).

Mueller, John, *Policy and Opinion in the Gulf War* (Chicago: University of Chicago Press, 1994).

———, "Public Support for Military Ventures Abroad," in John Norton Moore and Robert F. Turner, eds., *The Real Lessons of the Vietnam War: Reflections Twenty-Five Years after the Fall of Saigon* (Durham, NC: Carolina Academic Press, 2002).

———, *War, Presidents, and Public Opinion* (New York: John Wiley and Sons, 1973).

Murray, Shailagh, "Clinton, Obama to Back Vote to Cut off Funding for Troops in Iraq," *Washington Post* 2007, A04.

A National Security Strategy for a New Century, 1998, clinton2.nara.gov/WH/EOP/NSC/html/documents/nssr.pdf (accessed 2005).

National Strategy for Victory in Iraq, 2005, White House, http://www.whitehouse.gov/infocus/iraq/iraq_strategy_nov2005.html. (accessed January 2006).

Neilson, W., and J. Stowe, "A Further Examination of Cumulative Prospect Theory Parameterizations," *Journal of Risk and Uncertainty*, Vol. 24, No. 1 (2002), 31–46.

Neither Election nor Fighting in Fallujah Changes Public Attitudes on Iraq, 2004, Harris Poll #93, www.harrisinteractive.com/harris_poll/index.asp?PID=522 (accessed January 2006).

Nicholson, Michael, *Formal Theories of International Relations* (New York: Cambridge University Press, 1989).

Odean, Terrance, "Are Investors Reluctant to Realize Their Losses?," in Daniel Kahneman and Amos Tversky, eds., *Choices, Values, and Frames* (Cambridge: Cambridge University Press, 2000).

Overwhelming Support for Bush, Military Response But . . . American Psyche Reeling from Terror Attacks, 2001, Pew Research Center, www.pewtrusts.com/ideas/ideas_item.

cfm?content_item_id=749&content_type_id=18&issue_name=Public%20opin-ion%20and%20polls&issue=11&page=18&name=Public%20Opinion%20Polls%20and%20Survey%20Results#intro (accessed August 2005).

Page, Benjamin I., and Robert Y Shapiro, *The Rational Public: Fifty Years of Trends in Americans' Policy Preferences* (Chicago: University of Chicago Press, 1992).

Peake, Jeffrey S., "The Limits of Presidential Rhetoric: The Agenda-Setting Impact of Major Television Addresses," Paper presented at the Annual Meeting of the American Political Science Association 2003.

———, "Presidential Agenda Setting in Foreign Policy," *Political Research Quarterly*, Vol. 54, No. 1 (2001), 69–86.

Peterson, Paul E., "The President's Dominance in Foreign Policy Making," Political Science Quarterly, Vol. 109 (1994), pp. 215–234.

Pew Bush Leadership Approval Index, 2005, Pew Research Center, www.pewtrusts.com/pdf/PRC_terror_0705.pdf, www.pewtrusts.com/pdf/PRC_Bush_1005.pdf (accessed November 26 2005).

Pfiffner, James P., *The Strategic Presidency: Hitting the Ground Running* (Chicago: Dorsey, 1988).

Philippe, F., "Cumulative Prospect Theory and Imprecise Risk," *Mathematical Social Sciences*, Vol. 40, No. 3 (2000), 237–263.

Poll: Americans Taking Abramoff, Alito and Domestic Spying in Stride, 2006, Pew Research Center, www.pewtrusts.com/pdf/PRC_news_01106.pdf (accessed January 2006).

Post-Blix: Public Favors Force in Iraq, But . . . U.S. Needs More International Backing, 2003, Pew Research Center in association with Council on Foreign Relations, www.pewtrusts.com/pdf/vf_pew_research_international_backing.pdf (accessed December 3, 2005).

Quattrone, George A., and Amos Tversky, "Contrasting Rational and Psychological Analyses of Political Choice," *American Political Science Review*, Vol. 82, No. 3 (1988), 719–736.

Reiter, Dan, and Allan C. Stam, *Democracies at War* (Princeton, NJ: Princeton University Press, 2002).

Rove: Security Will Be Focus of 2006 Campaigns, 2006, CNN, www.cnn.com/2006/POLITICS/01/20/republicans.rove.ap/index.html (accessed January, 2006).

Russett, Bruce, *Controlling the Sword: The Democratic Governance of National Security* (Cambridge, MA: Harvard University Press, 1990).

Russett, Bruce, and Thomas W.Graham, "Public Opinion and National Security Policy: Relationships and Impacts," in Manus I. Midlarsky, ed., *Handbook of War Studies* (Ann Arbor: University of Michigan Press, 1989).

Schaub, Gary, "Deterrence, Compellence, and Prospect Theory," *Political Psychology*, Vol. 25, No. 3 (2004), 389–411.

Schmidt, U., "Reference Dependence in Cumulative Prospect Theory," *Journal of Mathematical Psychology*, Vol. 47, No. 2 (2003), 122–131.

Shane, Scott, "Bush's Speech on Iraq Echoes Analyst's Voice," *New York Times*, December 4 2005, 1.

Shannon, Vaughn P., "Norms Are What States Make of Them: The Political Psychology of Norm Violation," *International Studies Quarterly*, Vol. 44, No. 2 (2000), 293–316.

Shefrin, Hersh, and Meir Statman, "The Disposition to Sell Winners Too Early and Ride Losers Too Long: Theory and Evidence," *Journal of Finance*, Vol. 40, No. 3 (1985), 777–790.

Shiller, Robert J., "Human Behavior and the Efficiency of the Financial System," in John B. Taylor and Michael Woodford, eds., *Handbook of Macroeconomics* (North-Holland, 1999).

Simon, Herbert, "Rationality in Political Behavior," Political Psychology, Vol. 16 (1995), 45–61.

Simon, Herbert., "A Behavioral Model of Rational Choice," *Quarterly Journal of Economics*, Vol. 69 (1955), pp. 99–118.

———, "Human Nature in Politics: The Dialogue of Psychology with Political Science," *American Political Science Review*, Vol. 79 (1985), 293–304.

Slovic, Paul, Baruch Fischhof, and Sarah Lichtenstein, "Facts versus Fears: Understanding Perceived Risk," in Daniel Kahneman, Paul Slovic and Amos Tversky, eds., *Judgment under Uncertainty: Heuristics and Biases* (Cambridge: Cambridge University Press, 1982).

Snyder, Jack L., *Myths of Empire: Domestic Politics and International Ambition* (Ithaca, NY: Cornell University Press, 1991).

Sobel, Richard, *The Impact of Public Opinion on U.S. Foreign Policy since Vietnam* (New York: Oxford University Press, 2001).

Solid Majority Favors Congressional Troop Deadline, 2007, Pew Research Center, people-press.org/reports/pdf/313.pdf (accessed July 5, 2007).

Stevenson, Richard W., "President Makes It Clear: Phrase Is 'War on Terror'," *New York Times*, August 4, 2005.

Tajfel, H., and J. C. Turner, "The Social Identity Theory of Intergroup Behaviour," in S. Worchel and W. Austin, eds., *Psychology of Intergroup Relations* (Chicago: Nelson-Hall, 1986), 7–24.

Taliaferro, Jeffrey W., "Power Politics and the Balance of Risk: Hypotheses on Great Power Intervention in the Periphery," *Political Psychology*, Vol. 25, No. 2 (2004), 177–211.

———, "Quagmires in the Periphery: Foreign Wars and Escalating Commitment in International Conflict," *Security Studies*, Vol. 7, No. 3 (1998), 94–144.

Tedesco, John C., "Issue and Strategy Agenda-Setting in the 2000 Presidential Primaries," *American Behavioral Scientist*, Vol. 44, No. 12 (2001), 2048–2067.

Thaler, Richard H., Amos Tversky, Daniel Kahneman, and Alan Schwartz, "The Effect of Myopia and Loss Aversion on Risk Taking: An Experimental Test," *Quarterly Journal of Economics*, Vol. 112, No. 2 (1997), 647–661.

TIPP The Presidential Leadership Index, 2001–2004, TechnoMetrica Institute of Policy and Politics, www.tipponline.com/n_index/pli/2004/pl_1204.htm, www.tipponline .com/n_index/pli/2003/pl_1203.htm, www.tipponline.com/n_index/eoi/eo_102.htm (accessed August 2005).

Tversky, A., and D. Kahneman, "Advances in Prospect Theory—Cumulative Representation of Uncertainty," *Journal of Risk and Uncertainty*, Vol. 5, No. 4 (1992), 297–323.

———, "The Framing of Decisions and the Psychology of Choice," *Science*, Vol. 211 (1981), 453–458.

Tversky, Amos, and Daniel Kahneman, "Loss Aversion in Riskless Choice: A Reference-Dependent Model," *Quarterly Journal of Economics*, Vol. 106, No. 4 (1991), 1039–1061.

———, "Rational Choice and the Framing of Decisions," *Journal of Business*, Vol. 59, No. 4, Part 2 (1986), S251–S278.

Unusually High Interest in Bush's State of the Union, 2002 Pew Research Center.

Van Evera, Stephen, "Offense, Defense, and the Causes of War," *International Security*, Vol. 22, No. 4 (1998), 5–43.

Voeten, Erik, and Paul R. Brewer, "Public Opinion, the War in Iraq, and Presidential Accountability," *Journal of Conflict Resolution*, Vol. 50, No. 6 (2006), 809–830.

Wakker, P. P., and H. Zank, "A Simple Preference Foundation of Cumulative Prospect Theory with Power Utility," *European Economic Review*, Vol. 46, No. 7 (2002), 1253–1271.

Wakker, P., and A. Tversky, "An Axiomatization of Cumulative Prospect Theory," *Journal of Risk and Uncertainty*, Vol. 7, No. 2 (1993), 147–175.

Walt, Stephen M., "Beyond Bin Laden: Reshaping U.S. Foreign Policy," *International Security*, Vol. 26, No. 3 (2001), 56–78.

Waltz, Kenneth N., "Realist Thought and Neorealist Theory," in Charles W. Kegley, ed., *Controversies in International Relations Theory: Realism and the Neoliberal Challenge* (New York: St. Martin's Press, 1995).

Wang, X. T., "Self-Framing of Risky Choice," *Journal of Behavioral Decision Making*, Vol. 17, No. 1 (2004), 1–16.

Washington Post-ABC News Poll June 2005, *Washington Post*, www.washingtonpost.com/wp-dyn/content/article/2005/06/07/AR2005060700296.html, www.washingtonpost.com/wp-srv/politics/polls/postpoll050607.pdf (accessed August 2005).

Weaver, Ole, "European Integration and Security: Analysing French and German Discourses on State, Nation, and Europe," in David R. Howarth and Jacob Torfing, eds., *Discourse Theory in European Politics* (New York: Palgrave Macmillan, 2005).

Western, Jon, "Sources of Humanitarian Intervention," *International Security*, Vol. 26, No. 4 (2002), 112–142.

Weyland, Kurt, "The Political Fate of Market Reform in Latin America, Africa, and Eastern Europe," *International Studies Quarterly*, Vol. 42, No. 4 (1998), 645–673.

Whitesides, John, "Clinton's Iraq Vote Haunts Her on Campaign Trail," 2007, Reuters, www.reuters.com/article/topNews/idUSN2237058420070223 (accessed June 30, 2007).

Would You Favor or Oppose Having U.S. Forces Take Military Action against Iraq to Force Saddam Hussein from Power?, 2003, ABC News Poll. March 5–9, 2003. N = 1,032 adults nationwide. MoE ± 3, Fieldwork by TNS Intersearch, www.pollingreport.com/iraq9.htm (accessed August 2005).

Zakaria, Fareed, "Realism and Domestic Politics: A Review Essay," *International Security*, Vol. 17, No. 1 (1992), 177–198.

Index

About the Author

WOJTEK MACKIEWICZ WOLFE received his Ph.D. from the University of Colorado at Boulder, where he currently teaches as well as at the University of Denver's Graduate School of International Relations. This is his first book.